BONFIRE NIGHT IN LEWES
VARIOUS HISTORICAL ARTICLES COLLECTED AND COMPILED WITH ADDITIONAL ORIGINAL ITEMS

By BRIAN W PUGH

The last bonfire and firework display held in Lewes High Street
Monday 6 November 1905

Cover and Title Page Photo courtesy of
Edward Reeves, 159 High Street,
Lewes, BN7 1XU

First published in 2011

© Copyright 2011 Brian W Pugh

The right of Brian W Pugh to be identified as the author of this work has been asserted by him in accordance with the Copyright, Designs and Patents Act 1998. All rights reserved. No reproduction, copy or transmission of this publication may be made without written permission. No paragraph of this publication may be reproduced, copied or transmitted save with the written permission or in accordance with the provisions of the Copyright Act 1956 (as amended). Any person who does any unauthorised act in relation to this publication may be liable to criminal prosecution and civil claims for damage.

Paperback ISBN 9781908218643

Mobipocket/Kindle ISBN 9781908218650

ePub ISBN 9781908218667

MX Publishing Ltd, 335 Princess Park Manor, Royal Drive, London, N11 3GX

www.mxpublishing.co.uk

Cover design by Staunch
www.staunch.com

Lewes High Street outside the White Hart in the nineteenth century, the effigies can be seen top right.
Photo is on display at Anne of Cleves House, Southover High Street, Lewes.

DEDICATION

This book is dedicated to the Bonfire Boyes and Girls, past, present and the future.

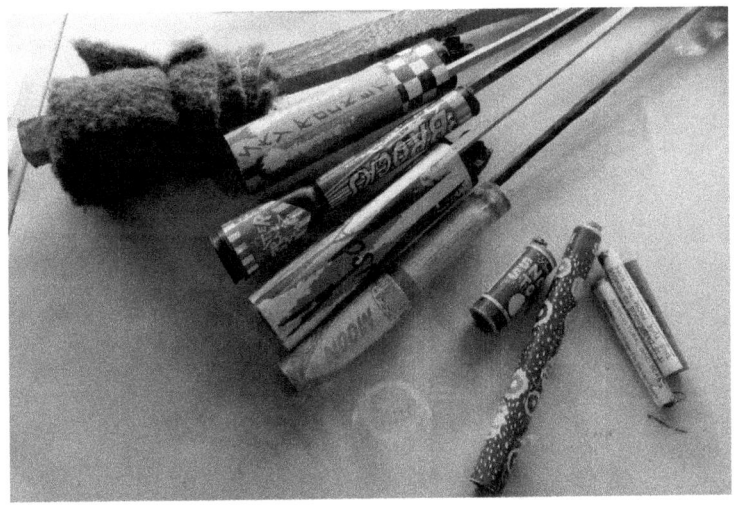

Rockets, rook scarers and torch on display at Anne of Cleves House, Southover High Street, Lewes.

INTRODUCTION

During the first week of November the usually sleepy East Sussex town of Lewes comes to life with the annual November 5th Celebrations. This is usually celebrated on the fifth, unless it falls on a Sunday, when it is then held on the Saturday. Over the years Lewes has become the Capital of Bonfire; of course other towns and villages carry out their own celebrations, but not on the scale of that at Lewes. There are numerous Bonfire Societies in Sussex with the bonfire season stating in September until late November, too many to include in this publication, so it concentrates only on the Lewes Celebrations.

It is hoped that through these following articles you can relive the celebrations of bygone years. They are collected here together for the first time and give an insight to how November 5th or Bonfire Night was seen in the eighteen hundreds. Also included is the complete chapter taken from *The Spirit of the Downs* by Arthur Beckett, and the articles written and privately published by Bert Munt and Simon O'Halloran. The other articles Lewes Bonfire Information, an introduction to Bert Munt, A Time Line and the winners of the Pioneer Cup and the Points Cup won at the Lewes Bonfire Council Fancy Dress Competition are by the author and Bonfire Societies of Lewes and List of Bonfire Societies: Existing and Previous are by David S. Bristow and the author. The Index has been compiled by David S. Bristow.

Pages 1 to 47 and 50 to 123, the pamphlets, have been transcribed and appear verbatim, so there is some spelling and punctuation that will appear to be incorrect.

ACKNOWLEGMENTS

I would like acknowledge Mrs Dorothy Philips (née Munt), sister of Bert, David Philips (nephew) and Christine Munt (niece) for their permission to publish *Lewes Bonfire* by Bert Munt. Also thanks to Esme Evans (Sussex Past, Barbican Library Lewes) and those at Lewes Library for their help, Roger Meyer (Secretary of Lewes Bonfire Council); John Winter (Chairman Borough B.S.); David Quinn (Waterloo B.S.); Bruce Wadey (South Street B.S.), Keith Austin, Geoff Isted, Roger Bristow, Barry Jackman, John and Christine Armitage, East Sussex Records Office, Maltings, Lewes, Cathy Bridges (Battel Bonfire Boyes), John Cleary (Clapham & Patching Bonfire Club), Richard Cooper (Littlehampton B.S.), Alan Martin (Marsfield B.S.), Mark Woods (Vines Cross B.S.), Carol Watts (Uckfield Bonfire & Carnival Society), Ben West (Merrie Harriers), Jez Southgate (Frog & Duck Society), Sally Gravett (Firle B.S.), Eric Crouch (Ewhurst & Staplecross B.S.), Sam Moon (Robertsbridge B.S.) and Chichester & Tunbridge Wells Libraries.

My extreme gratitude and thanks go to Peter Martin for the use of the Cliffe Bonfire Society Archives and to David S. Bristow for supplying from his own collection newspaper transcripts, information about existing and previous societies, compiling the Persons Index and proof reading. And thanks to all those that gave me support and encouragement to compile this book.

I have endeavoured to locate Simon O'Halloran to gain permission to include his privately printed booklet, *Bonfire in Lewes* and Arthur Beckett to include the chapter from *The Spirit of the Downs*, but to no avail. So I would like to acknowledge both as the authors.

CONTENTS

Page	
1.	*The Domestick Intelligence* (No. 39) by Benjamin Harris, Tuesday 18 November 1679.
3.	*Observations on the Doings in Lewes on the Evening of the Fifth of November 1846, with a few words to parties interested*. By An Old Inhabitant, 1846, attributed to Mark Anthony Lower. [Printed by Geo. P. Bacon, Sussex Advertiser Office, Lewes, MDCCCXLVI].
12.	*Bonfires in the past: a retrospect* by A Lewes Bonfire Boy. Reprinted from the *East Sussex News* of 7 November 1879, *with Additional Interesting Particulars* by William Banks. [Lewes: W. Banks, Antiquarian House, Station Street and Farncombe & Co., Printers, Lewes].
23.	*Lewes and its Bonfires*, 1899, from *A Guide to Lewes: The Castle and the Priory* by John Sawyer, pp 75-76. [Ringmer: Frank W. Burgess, 1899].
26.	Chapter XVIII, *A South Down Saturnalia*, from *The Spirit of the Downs* by Arthur Beckett, pp 204-225, [London: Methuen & Co., 1909].
48.	Introduction to Sydney Albert (Bert) Munt.
50.	*Bonfire* by Bert Munt, 1958.
70.	*Bonfires in Lewes* by Simon O'Halloran, 1967.
119.	*Lewes Bonfires 1908, 1909 & 1910* by Annette Philly Verrell, [Historian Vol. 7, No. 6, September 1987.
124.	Lewes Bonfire Society Information.
126.	*A Time Line of Bonfire in Lewes*.
169.	Lewes Bonfire Council Fancy Dress Competition.
172.	Bonfire Societies in Lewes 1845-to date.
174.	List of Existing and Previous Bonfire Societies.
180.	The Modern Version of *Bonfire Prayers*.
181.	*Gunpowder Plot* by Vernon Scannell.
182.	*The Lewes Rouser* by Squib.

183. *1605 and Since by W.C.*, 1911.
184. *Sussex By The Sea* by William Ward-Higgs, 1907.
186. *Sussex Won't Be Druv* by W. Victor Cook.
187. Sources and Further Reading.
189. About the Author.
191. Index of Persons.

Goggles worn during procession and bonfire and powder spoons on display at Anne of Cleves House, Southover High Street, Lewes.

THE DOMESTICK INTELLIGENCE
(No. 39) by Benjamin Harris.
Tuesday, November 18, 1679. A London News-sheet.

Lewes in Sussex, Nov. 5. This day was celebrated here with extraordinary Solemnity, there being a Procession not unworthy taking notice of. In the first place went a company of young men armed with swords and muskets, pikes &c. like a company of soldiers; next several pictures were carried upon long poles, the first being a Jesuit represented with a bloody sword and a pistol, with this inscription: "Our Religion is Murder, Rapine and Rebellion". The second was the picture of a Frier and a Jesuit wantonly dallying with a Nun, the Devil looking from behind a curtain, and saying "I will spoil no sport, my dear children". The third was the picture of two devils bringing a triple crown to the Pope, with these words "Hail Holy Father". There was a fourth likewise; but the former are most material. To every one of these were verses spoken as they passed by. Just before the Pope marched Guy Faux with his dark Lanthorn, being booted and spurred after the Old Fashion, and wearing a vizard with a wonderful long nose. Next comes the Pope with his Cross Keys, Crosier Staffe and other Fopperies, having his train borne up by several of his clergy, being saluted as he passed by with a copy of verses. Next followed the cardinals in their caps, with the rest of the clergy secular and regular, having wonderful long beards, and a string of beads about their middle, which they told as they went along. Behind these went the nuns. But last of all comes the ghost of Sir Edmunbury Godfrey represented by a person in black cloaths, and a shirt all bloody, and his face painted so white that he seemed dead rather than alive, before whom went a person carrying a bloody sword in his hand who sometimes looking back would seem to be greatly affrighted at the sight of him. There were between twenty and thirty boys with vizards, and two or three who had their faces painted after an antick manner, one whereof carried Holy Water in a tin pot, sprinkling the people with a bottle-brush. In this manner they having carried his Holiness through the Town and Streets adjacent, at night, after they had first degraded him, they committed him to the flames. This being an example not unworthy to be imitated upon the like occasion, it was judged meet to give publick notice there-of.

******

THE BURNING OF RICHARD WOODMAN AND NINE OTHER PROTESTANT MARTYRS BEFORE THE STAR INN, LEWES
From the Engraving by Mr. F. Colvin, Lewes

Observations on the Doings in Lewes on the Evening of the Fifth of November 1846 With A Few Words to Parties Interested
By
An Old Inhabitant

OBSERVATIONS, &c.

"Lust and licentiousness
Creep in the minds and marrow of our youth;
That 'gainst the stream of *Virtue* they may strive
And drown themselves in *riot*!"

"Slaves and fools
Pluck the grave wrinkled senate from the beach
And minister in their steads!"
SHAKESPEARE.

Another anniversary of the Fifth of November is past; it was accompanied by all the usual disgusting parade of disguises, bludgeons and riot; the burning of tar-barrels, thirty or upwards in number; fireballs, with rockets and the general description of fireworks. The whole trade of the High-street virtually at an end about six o'clock; and by seven, or soon after, the first tar-barrels made their appearance and continued till half-past eleven, and it was half-past twelve before the mob dispersed and the remains of the fire put out.

This is but a repetition of what has been witnessed in Lewes for a series of years on the evening of this day. The streets are taken possession of by a mob led by a large number of disguised fellows (who, I expect, when not disguised, call themselves *"gents"*) and a more ungentlemanly set of ruffians it would be difficult to find, each armed with a large bludgeon, parading the streets, superintending the lighting tar barrels, and witnessing their being dragged, lighted, from one end of the High-street to the other, with an occasional outburst of—

    "Happy land, happy land!"
 or

  "Rule Britannia, Britannia rules the waves!"
  "Britons never will be slaves," &c.

"Happy" indeed must any land be under the control of such a set of ignorant raggamuffins. And where can be a more lamentable or disgusting sight, than to look upon a large body of human beings in a state of savage excitement, "slaves" to the worst feelings and impulses of which their nature is susceptible? And yet, such a sight might have been witnessed for hours last night in the High-street of Lewes.

We have been told for years past, that, if the matter were left alone, it would die *a natural death*. What interference took place last night? What attempt had been made to *"destroy the harmony of the evening"* or to prevent any of the disgraceful and degrading scenes of former years, except a very modest and proper exhortation by "A Young Inhabitant" to the young men of the town to forbear the annoyance to their respectable and peaceful neighbours, and to retire to the Cliffe Hill, where they might enjoy themselves to the utmost with their tar-barrels, fireworks and noise?

We have been told, that if no notice is taken, no mischief will be done. Let any individual only be *suspected* by the mob as unfavourable to them, and forthwith he is a marked man—if he venture among them he is personally ill-used and insulted, or his house beset, with tar-barrels drawn to the front of it and burnt with all the disgusting accompaniments so well understood by this *band of heroes*.

And all this is taking place in the middle of the nineteenth century and carried on by the enlightened youth who have been born and educated since my Lord Brougham's Schoolmaster has been abroad. Is it possible that this can be one of the results of a superior method of teaching the people? Here are not one or two individual instances, but fifties and hundreds who, in their ignorance, finding their power uncontrolled, set the law at defiance and out-brave the constituted authorities.

Surely there must be something wrong about this? Either this boasted education has fallen wofully short of its design, or the authorities are scarcely firm enough in carrying out the powers entrusted to them: perhaps the truth lies between the two.

Before making the appeal I am about to do, to the higher powers for their interference, I am extremely anxious that they may perfectly understand the position of the peaceably disposed inhabitants of the town of Lewes. It has been said that the magistrate cannot act without a request being made to them in some form or other. Here is a difficulty, and so long as things are as they are, so long will this difficulty exist. Send a memorial round the town to-morrow morning, for signature, requesting the magistrates to take the necessary measures to prevent a recurrence of the scenes of last night, and it would be found that many highly respectable inhabitants would refuse to sign it—not because *they do not feel* the impropriety of the proceedings—not because they do not feel a *pressing necessity* existing for doing away with the nuisance—but, from the want of a proper moral courage, and from a fear that their property or premises may be injured by the hand of the malicious villain, or perhaps the midnight incendiary. This is not an overdrawn picture. I know several instances, and have no doubt that many more exist; and this in some measure accounts, for what may appear to those not knowing the truth, like a feeling of apathy on the part of the inhabitants of Lewes.

I believe no one can attribute to the magistracy, an insensibility to their responsibilities, nor can it be possible that men of such high moral feeling can be restrained by any thing like fear from fulfilling the duties imposed by their office.

I would most respectfully call on his Grace the Duke of Richmond, as the *head of the magistracy*, both by his countenance and advice, to aid the Lewes bench of magistrates in any measures they may propose, in order to quell the unlawful and riotous proceedings which annually disgrace the town of Lewes, on the fifth of November.

I most earnestly request the Right Hon. the Earl of Chichester, and the other magistrates constituting the Lewes bench, having the long period of a year before them, to give the whole matter their most serious consideration; and I trust, after due deliberation, they will feel themselves imperatively called upon to adopt such decisive measures as will certainly prevent even an attempt on the part of those usually concerned in the unseemly proceedings in Lewes—to carry on, during the night of the fifth of November in the next year, any such dangerous and disgraceful riots as for years past have been suffered—and I trust they will find very many of the inhabitants willing to render them every assistance in their power; and I would remind them, that last night, one of their body was hustled and knocked down, and maltreated in a most infamous manner and his life endangered, by this *quiet mob*, who "*intend no mischief.*"

Within a few weeks of the first of November, several hints were thrown out as to the propriety of the chief officers of the Borough interfering: of what earthly use is their interference? As conservators of the peace, by the operation of the Constabulary Act, they are rendered utterly powerless, and the power taken from them is placed in the hands of the magistrates, the chief constable, and the body of men under his control; and I think I may say, that if the chief constable and all his posse were called into Lewes on the nigh of the fifth of November, to attempt to quell the riots, they would be of *non-effect*, and it would be placing their lives in jeopardy without the slightest chance of good arising from their presence, or aid from their exertions. I beg it to be understood, that in the fore going remarks, not the slightest reflection is intended to be cast upon the chief constable, or any of those under him; but from want of numerical strength, and a habit of acting together as a body, conceive they would be wholly unable to withstand an infuriated mob similar to that assembled on the fifth of November; and yet I would remind the magistracy that the town of Lewes is taxed annually to the amount of about £300, for the support of a body of men, wholly inefficient in a case of the greatest need.

With respect to the chief officers of the Borough, I should add that I am convinced no men feet more anxious, and I am sure efforts on their part will ever be wanting to guard against mischief; and they were, I believe, last night actively engaged in various part of the town, to the utmost that their individual exertions would allow.

I would remind the Commissioners acting under the 46

Geo., 3, commonly called the "Town Act, that there is a clause in page 16, inflicting a penalty not exceeding forty shillings, for assisting or abetting in making any bonfire; or letting off, firing, making, selling, &c., any crackers, squibs, or other fireworks." Are the whole body of commissioners so forgetful of the oath they have taken to execute and perform the several powers and authorities reposed in them as commissioners, as to suffer this law to pass as a dead letter?

I would now address a few words to the inhabitants themselves, that is the peaceably disposed, and right thinking portion. Let all endeavour before another year is at an end to rescue this ancient and respectable borough from the disgrace to which, for some years, it has been obnoxious; by earnestly appealing to the heads of families, tradesmen, and the inhabitants generally, to prevent by all means in their power, those over whom they have any control, from taking part in the disgusting and illegal proceedings, and to lend efficient aid to die magistrates in any exertions they may make for this purpose. And further, I put it to their reason and common sense, as well as to their better feelings, whether this conduct (such as can be found in no other town) should not, for the credit and respectability of Lewes, at once be brought to an end.

If there are any, who from religious prepossessions or otherwise, feel themselves called upon to commemorate the anniversary of Gunpowder Plot, I am sure they will see the reasonableness of confining their rejoicings to their own premises, without annoyance or danger to their neighbours.

There is one point to which I would advert, and that is, to what extent the town may be injured by these injudicious and improper proceedings on the Fifth of November?

That the trade suffer I am fully convinced. Commercial men and others, who have been in the habit of stopping at Lewes, finding what was likely to occur, have gone to Brighton to avoid the nuisance; this *did* occur yesterday, and the party returned by rail this morning to transact business.

There is still another point of great importance.—Many persons are looking forward with considerable anxiety, to see whether any and what good will result to the town from the railway. It hat been said, that when the "*Keymer Branch*" shall be completes many persons will prefer a *quiet*(?) town like Lewes for a place of residence, to Brighton or other large and gay watering places—and as a place of sojourn for convalescent persons, it is likely to be preferred to the sea-side; but, who would not, however much they might feel inclined to reside in Lewes, immediately take the alarm on seeing the accounts of the excesses committed here on the Fifth of November, and however much good the railway *might* do to Lewes, the inhabitants themselves prevent it by a want of peaceable and orderly conduct?

To the young men of the town I would say a few words:— It was with pity and with shame I last night beheld the assassin-like and un-English disguise and mask resorted to among you to avoid recognition. What can be more cowardly? Is this the mode of action for the open-hearted, open-handed, manly youth of England? One would almost expect next to see the *poison cup* and the *stiletto*. Never, oh! never let these things occur again, but whatever opposition you may in future feel yourselves called upon to show, throw away the shelter of the *Italian Bravo*, and appear in your true characters as Englishmen, who can never feel ashamed of being known when engaged honestly and in a good cause. The time appears to have arrived when a feeling of disgust pervades the minds of the respectable and right thinking portion of the inhabitants of Lewes; and I implore you to give your aid to any efforts which may be made to quell the riotous proceedings of the Fifth of November. Surely the motives adduced by "A Young Inhabitant" should have been sufficient; but I am fully aware of the power of example, and when I know the nephews, cousins, and connections of some of the principal inhabitants in the town were among you, and the legal, mercantile, landed and other interests were fairly represented by those who were encouraging the disgraceful scenes enacted last night by their presence openly and undisguisedly—some of them for hours employed in discharging rockets of a size and power really dangerous—I can hardly blame some of you for acting with such countenance; but I would urge upon you most seriously the folly (to call it no worse) of your conduct, and upon due and mature consideration I hope and trust your good feelings and common sense will dictate a different course of conduct in future.

A very large amount of property in Lewes is insured in something over a dozen offices, and I believe but very few of them know the extra risk to which they are exposed during the night of the Fifth of November; when the discovery is made by them, I am certain they will, without an exception, memorialise the magistrates to prevent a recurrence of this burning of tar-barrels, &c., and thereby free them from such extra risk arising from the wanton and illegal conduct of the inhabitants themselves: and I would beg to remind the magistrates that by far the major part of this burning tar-barrels, &c., takes place immediately in front of the County Hall, where last night might have been seen the remains of three, four, or five tar-barrels at one time piled on each other, sending the flames and sparks higher than the roof of the building—and this building is the depository of the whole of the County Records, and *not one* room or, even a closet, *fire-proof* in the place. Surely these facts alone should operate to call the most serious attention of the magistrates to the matter, and act as an extra incentive to their exertions to stop these riots and fires.

Having made a few observations upon the several points which I consider necessary, and having addressed a few words to those parties who I believed to be most interested, I will conclude by stating my firm conviction, that if *each party here addressed*, after most seriously reflecting upon the various matters placed before them, will but follow the dictates of their consciences—and their good feelings—and do their duty to the utmost in the several situations in which they may be placed, there can be no difficulty in ridding the town of Lewes of this abominable and disgraceful nuisance, and I am convinced that, on the Fifth of November, 1847, Lewes may be as free from annoyance as any other large and respectable town in the kingdom.

AN OLD INHABITANT.

Lewes, November 6th, 1846.

Some persons reading these observations may object to their being put forth anonymously. Feeling that they contain the truth, my only motive for withholding my name is that individually I possess so little influence among my fellow townsmen, that it might be considered presumption on my part to have published it.
Nov. 6, 1846
THE AUTHOR

******

Bonfires in the Past:
A Retrospect
By A Lewes Bonfire Boy
With
Additional Interesting Particulars
By William Banks

Whether or not the custom of commemorating Guy Fawkes' infamous Plot originated in Lewes at the early period we are sometimes asked to believe, it is evident from historical records that its existence extends over at least a century and a half. But the form and scale of the carnival, as well as the circumstances under which it has been carried out, have changed with succeeding generations. It must not be. supposed, for instance, that because during the last twenty years the proceedings have not been attended with opposition that such was the case in former days; or that because Lewes can now boast of four well-organised bonfire societies, who carry out magnificent displays and receive the favourable consideration and support of the majority of the inhabitants as well as the manifest approval of the "authorities," that such were the characteristics of the demonstrations before the commencement of the second half of the present century. Very little, authentic information respecting the early history of the carnival is obtainable, but, if report deserves credence, the general interest in the fiery festival—especially during the reign of James II.—was as intense as that attaching to it in later years. It is said that none of the public spectacles of that period interested the common people so much as the one with which they had a few years before been familiar, and which they now, after a long interval, gazed upon once more—the burning of the Pope's effigy. This once popular pageant included a figure by no means resembling the rude representations of Guy Fawkes which are generally paraded on each recurring 5th November. They were made of wax with great skill and adorned, at considerable expense, with robes and a tiara. The effigy was mounted on a chair resembling that in which clerical dignitaries are still, at some high festivals, borne through St. Peter's to the High Altar. "His Holiness," was usually accompanied by a long retinue of Cardinals and Jesuits. At his car stood a buffoon, disguised as a devil, with horns and tail. No rich and zealous Protestant begrudged his guinea on such an occasion, and, if rumour can be trusted, the cost of the procession alone was not less than £1,000. After this representative Pope had been borne for some time in state over the heads of the multitude he was committed to the flames amid great acclamations. As years advanced, interest in the affair, from some unexplained cause, lessened, until at length little more than the lighting and keeping up of huge fires constituted the entire programme of the proceedings. After the first twenty years of the present century, however, expectations of a revival were not disappointed, but no sooner was this increased vitality brought about than mischievous acts to private property began to be perpetrated, followed in their train by incendiary fires and other lawless incidents. The Brightonians were at this time celebrated for their anti-popery exhibitions on the Marine-parade and in the year 1829 was first introduced into Lewes the system of dragging lighted tar-barrels through the streets, as well as the use of fireballs and dangerous combustibles. Cautions were issued by the local authorities with a view of suppressing this dangerous custom, but their efforts simply met with ridicule and defiance. Many of the more law-abiding enthusiasts of the Cliffe lit fires on the Cliffe-hill, Mount Caburn being selected as the general rendezvous. As an interesting incident it might be mentioned that at this last mentioned site the son of Mr. John Hillman, merchant, met with an accident of a somewhat serious character from the incautious use of a powder horn. In 1831 the proceedings were carried out with greater energy than ever. Throughout the night the streets were filled with boys who let off squibs with impunity, to the great annoyance of the inhabitants and owners of property in particular. Another unsuccessful attempt to defeat the aims of the "boys" occurred in the following year, but the four successive anniversaries passed off without serious disturbance. The celebration of 1838 is distinguished for the rioting which then prevailed amongst a section of "elevated" roughs. Several of the offenders were apprehended by the police and having been tried before the Magistrates penalties of £15 and under were inflicted. This was the occasion, too, on which the late Mr. Whitfeld, whilst in the discharge of his Magisterial duties, had a pretty sharp encounter with a party who had a barrel on the Cliffe Bridge. Owing to the bitter feeling which existed free fights with bludgeons went on whenever a crowd collected and besides the serious harm occasioned by the *melées* a considerable amount of damage was done to property.

The celebration of 1839, although attended with a general letting off of squibs, &c., and the dragging of tar barrels through the streets, was free from any serious accident or mischief. The Coombe was lit up with a blazing bonfire, which had a very pleasing effect in the distance, and the lieges at Southover were entertained with a merry peal on the church bells. The demonstration of 1840 passed off in an equally peaceful manner, but in the following year the police endeavoured to prevent a continuance of the illegal custom of drawing lighted barrels through the town and the dangerous practice of throwing fire balls about. Parties engaged in the commission of the former act were armed with formidable bludgeons and on the interference of the police, whose muster had been largely augmented by the swearing in of special constables, general melees occurred. The "guardian angels" were severely beaten and Supt. Flanagan was struck heavily on his head with a boulder, knocked down with a bludgeon and trampled upon. The affray was waged fiercely and lasted a long time, many persons narrowly escaping injury which if inflicted might have proved fatal. Upwards of twenty of the principal transgressors were captured and tried at the ensuing assizes, the result of which was they were sent to prison for terms ranging from a fortnight to two months. At the expiration of their sentences they were required to enter into their own recognisances in sums of £100 and £60 to keep the peace for two years. Those convicted expiated their crimes with the spirit of martyrs.

An agreeable contrast to the observance just referred to was that which marked the anniversary in 1842. On the whole, it is said, the exhibition was tame and spiritless and there was a comparatively trifling display of squibs, fireballs and tar barrels, of which latter only two were brought out in the course of the evening. There not being the slightest disposition to excess on the part of those participating in the carnival the police did not interfere. A novelty, however, was introduced into the display in the shape of a band of music playing through the streets, accompanied by a large concourse of people. This was, probably, the first time a band of music was used at these annual demonstrations, "Rule Britannia" being the favourite air.

Passing on to 1843 we find not the slightest attempt at mischief-making identified with the celebration, and the same may be said of the two succeeding years. Between this period and 1846 exertions were made to induce the bonfire boys to remove their fun and frolic to some less dangerous place than the public streets, but they stoutly refused to act upon the suggestion. Early in the evening of the 5th November, 1846, a mob of several hundreds of men and boys, the majority being in disguise and armed with clubs and staves, paraded the streets, and shortly after tar barrels were dragged through the streets with great rapidity, to the affright of the inhabitants. This scene of lawlessness was diversified in many ways, but no actual mischief occurred till ten o'clock. At this hour the infuriated mob proceeded to the residence of Mr. Blackman, a popular and generally esteemed magistrate, and immediately in front of his house they piled up a number of barrels and set them on fire. The flames rose to a great height almost instantly, and created much alarm among the inmates of his house. Fearing the safety of his property and anxious to allay the fears of his household, Mr. Blackman went out and mildly, but firmly, desired the mob to disperse. The worthy Magistrate's remarks were received with derisive jeers, and fresh fuel was piled to increase the flames. Finding his efforts futile Mr. Blackman attempted to take one of the ringleaders into custody, and had nearly succeeded in doing so, when he received a violent blow over the eye with a bludgeon and was felled to the ground, it was at first thought, lifeless. He was subsequently taken home in a state of insensibility, and slowly recovered after much suffering. The demonstration that night did not cease till further riot and much wilful damage had been committed.

Some time prior to the 5th in 1847 the Magistrates avowed their intention of stopping the celebration, and their decision created considerable consternation. The police served summonses on all the respectable tradesmen and others, requiring their attendance at the County-hall to be sworn in as special constables for the occasion. The strongest disinclination to serve was manifested by many and a private meeting of the parties summoned was held at the Star Hotel, at which a memorial was drawn up suggesting that the means proposed were not the best to effect the object, inasmuch as if special constables were employed private feeling and interest would effectually check exertion to apprehend the offenders. The memorialists, therefore, asked the Magistrates to withdraw the summonses. The petition, which received 108 signatures out of a possible 170, was duly presented to the Magistrates, before a, crowded Court, by a deputation, consisting of Messrs. H. Saxby, E. Chatfield, G. Wood, Morris, Wille, jun., and T. Hillman, but the Bench expressed their inability to accede to the desire of the petitioners, and, with a few exceptions, the whole of those summoned were sworn in. The Chairman said that the Magistrates had taken every precaution, and were in communication with the Secretary of State with a view to stop the demonstration. The bonfire boys were thereby at once aroused to action. The special constables held another meeting on the night of the 4th, and on their way to the meeting house they were assaulted by large groups of defiant young men, who were located at different parts of the High-street. It required no great foresight to arrive at the conclusion that the Gunpowder Plot anniversary of that year was to be celebrated in the early morning instead of the night of the 5th, and Lord Chichester and Sir Henry Shiffner, Bart, (magistrates), being informed of the fact, quickly arrived in the town. About eleven o'clock on the night of the 4th tar barrels were lighted in several byeways and disturbances went on in many streets, but Captain Mackay and a large force were on the alert, and, after having quietly fastened a chain to the railings on each side of the road near Keere-street they betook themselves to ambush in Rotten Bow, should the threatening "Boys" attempt to carry out their plans. Shortly after twelve down St. Ann's-hill came a blazing tar barrel, drawn or surrounded by a body of seventy or eighty men, who, little anticipating any opposition, were stopped by the chain, over which several of them stumbled. The police rushed out on the rioters and a severe scuffle ensued, the result being that nearly a dozen of the ring-leaders were captured and lodged in durance vile. The morning of the 5th broke upon an excited people in Lewes, the "boys" still exhibiting tokens of resistance. At mid-day about 100 of the A Division, London Police arrived. At dusk they were concentrated in front of the County-hall, ready for any emergency. The town was divided into districts, in each of which bodies of "specials," carrying staves, took up their rendezvous. As the evening approached the crowds in the streets began to thicken and squibs and crackers were discharged in abundance. No opposition was offered to this beyond a vain but vigilant watch by the police to discover the parties. By eight o'clock the crowd had very greatly increased, and fireworks were being let off with impunity.

Soon after the mail gig from Brighton passed the County-hall at a furious rate, the driver vainly endeavouring to stop the animal, which had become frightened by a rocket. Onward it dashed at a rapid pace and inclining slightly to the right ended its course by coming into violent contact with a window at the corner of St. Mary's-lane. The poor driver was pitched out of the vehicle and much injured and another man was run over and severely bruised. In the meantime the Magistrates came to the determination to clear the streets. Lord Chichester read the Riot Act on the steps of the County-hall, and then, having delivered a brief address, allowed five minutes for the populace to disperse. Very few of the assembled throng, however, attempted to leave; the multitude were therefore charged and driven away by the A Division. The streets were by this means cleared. Several of the police were seriously hurt in the fray and on the following morning previous to their departure for London they were mercilessly stigmatised and hooted. Several evenings after the "Guys" availed themselves of the inactivity of the police (the latter having been instructed not to interpose) to roll tar barrels about the town and to fire off their store of squibs, and on one of these evenings there was as much commotion in the High-street as if it had been the Fifth of November of former years. Parties who had publicly manifested their hostility to the celebration had the windows of their houses broken and various other excesses were indulged in. Ultimately, however, tranquility was restored.

It was evident from the first that any step compelling submission by force would not be effectual and it was now seriously considered whether a compromise would not prove advantageous. The chief officers (Messrs. Smart and Neal) waited upon the Magistrates a few days previous to the 5th in the following year and asked that the custody of the town should be left in their hands. Acting upon this suggestion and having accepted the aid of the county constabulary arrangements for the event were duly made, it being understood that the constables were determined that no tar barrels should be brought into use, no fireballs thrown about, or any parties permitted to perambulate the streets in disguise. With the support and assistance of the headboroughs and some of the leading inhabitants a committee of tradesmen was formed with the object of celebrating the anniversary out of the town. Mr. John Ellman kindly offered the use of the Wallands Estate, which was gratefully accepted, and the necessary preliminaries having been completed the inhabitants were invited to assemble on the Wallands. A grand display was here carried out in the presence of several thousands of spectators, the fête passing off in a most satisfactory manner, and the constables were warmly thanked or the judicious steps they had taken. The plans pursued on this occasion were adopted on the recurring anniversary, and the whole arrangements were attended with the same signal success. Here may be noted the introduction of the famous twopenny squibs which gained for the manufacturer, the late Mr. F. Beeching, of Lewes, a universal reputation amongst participators in the carnival.

We now come to 1850, one of the most important years in the annals of "bonfirism" in Lewes. It was at this time the Pope renewed a determined attempt to embrace England in his superstitious grasp and it led the inhabitants to give a willing consent to the appropriation of the streets from one end of the town to the other for the full manifestation of Protestant feeling. A tremendous fire—far greater than we are accustomed to see now a days—was lit in the main street of the Cliffe, another in front of the County-hall and a third on Cliffe hill. Squibs and rockets were fired in great profusion, tar barrels were drawn through the thoroughfares, and the greatest enthusiasm everywhere prevailed. At midnight a tar barrel was ignited near the spot where the Papists were wont to light the fagot and burn to death their unyielding Protestant brethren, and although three centuries had elapsed since these dreadful occurrences this event vividly brought back the horrors which were associated with them. It may be of interest to mention the names of the victims in Lewes of Popish persecution. They are Carver, Harland, Oswald, Ovington, Read, Wood, Miles, Woodman, Stephens, Maynard, Hoffman, Morris and his mother, Burgess, Ashdown, and Grover's wives. Ever since 1850 the streets have been made the centre of the demonstrations, and if the affair is confined to the "Lewes Boys" there is not much fear of anything going wrong. Whilst remarking on the history of, the "1851 celebration" in Lewes, it should, be stated that the "Guernsey" style of dress came into general vogue, and it was in the same year that the editor of a local paper, who had made himself obnoxious to the "Boys," shared the "honours" of conflagration in effigy.

The "celebrationists" of the Cliffe formed themselves into a distinct society, about this period. The Commercial Square Society was established in 1855 or '56 and the Waterloo a year later; and although they have, each been subjected to a good deal of opposition and passed through many, vicissitudes, they now hold proud and conspicuous positions and carry out imposing demonstrations each year. About 1865 the Bonfire Boys' Court Milliner appeared on the scene, and by her wonderful perspicacity in the way of taste a trifling business has now assumed very large proportions, and the fruits of her handiwork find numerous patrons from all parts of Sussex and in some of the adjacent counties. In 1872 the efforts of the Court milliner were supplemented in another-direction by the introduction of Messrs. Brocks' illumination lights and since this period the effect of the processions has been thereby materially heightened. Three years later the ingeniously manufactured gauze wire eye protectors were imported by W. Banks, pyrotecnist, and the very extensive demand for them is an invincible proof of their great utility. To those familiar with the scene at Lewes on this particular day of the year it always looks the same in every respect, and if it were not for the continual introduction of some new blood it is probable the affair would have died out years ago, but to delight in this annual carnival seems "bred in the bone" of Lewes boys. They seem all to take to it naturally. On bonfire nights scores of even babes in arms may be seen in the assembled throng, with a view, probably, to encourage a taste for a more active interest in after years. There is no denying the fact that one night in each year the town of Lewes is handed over to mob law, and the town presents a singular spectacle of organised disorder. The townspeople evidently approve of the spectacle or it would not be permitted, and it is unfair not to give the "boys" credit for generally carrying out their arrangements in a good spirit and studiously avoiding any mischief to property and person. The writer is indebted to Mr. W. Banks, of Lewes, from whose documents many of the foregoing particulars are taken.

******

The Cliffe Martyrs Banner at Cliffe High Street, Lewes.

******

A Guide to Lewes: The Castle and the Priory
By
John Sawyer
Published by Frank W. Burgess of Ringmer in 1899

Lewes and its Bonfires

"While Lewes, blazing through the Shades of night."
Dr. Mantell.

Not in direct or special commemoration of the death of the Martyrs in the streets of the County Town, as might at first be imagined, but professedly as an expression of detestation of the treachery perpetrated by
"Guy Fawkes, the Prince of Sinisters,"
the good people of Lewes and district, for miles round, assemble in their thousands on each successive 5th of November to hold high Carnival before the County Hall, and make a night of it. What with professions music, banners, fancy costumes, masks, bonfires, tar barrels, torches, fireworks, including the celebrated "Corporation Rousers," the "Boys" of Lewes and Southover keep it up and generally manage to combine by means of effigy, tableaux, or oration some allusions to matters national or topical, with the inevitable pronouncements upon the history of the Plot, the aims of the Pope, and the constancy of the Protestant Martyrs. Would it be heretical to suggest that whilst the Commemoration is, in theory, essentially a protest against Popery and Ritualism, that the Bonfires Boys probably are suite as anxious in practice to secure an opportunity to indulge in a little innocent relaxation, to figure dressed in "gorgeous way" and generally to have "a good time," as to keep in memory those tragic events or that happy deliverance which led originally to the demonstration being held.

No one should miss the opportunity of seeing, for once at least, the Lewes Carnival, which in extent and brilliancy throws into the shade every other Sussex celebration. The "four well-organized bonfire societies," of which the town can boast, carry out a really magnificent programme on each recurring anniversary of "Guy Fawkes' infamous Plot." The members of the societies have since 1851 adopted the "Guernsey" style of dress. The arrangements are carried out in admirable fashion, and as has been well said "the town presents a singular spectacle of organized disorder." [1] It was not always thus, the author of these pages, who was younger then, remembers when the arrival of the 5th of November was dreaded in Lewes; and it was quite a relief to find the celebration pass off without a disturbance. In 1838 there was serious rioting followed by magisterial investigations and the infliction of heavy fines. In 1839, when "the Coombe was lit up with a blazing bonfire," all passed off well. 1840 was also quiet, but in 1841 a serious affray took place, and twenty of the leaders were tried at the Assizes and imprisoned for terms ranging from a fortnight to two months "hard," as well as having to enter into heavy recognisances to keep the peace for two years. For a few years things quieted down. In 1846 disturbances recommenced and a magistrate (Mr. Blackman) was nearly killed. In 1847 a terrible affray took place, the Riot Act was read and the streets cleared by the police, some members of the force being seriously hurt. The authorities finding themselves powerless to suppress the celebration by force a compromise was arrived at and the carnival held out of me town on the Wallands' Estate in 1848 and '49, but in 1850 when the Papal Invasion of England was resolved on, the fire of Protestant zeal flared up so briskly that a real anti-papal demonstration was held in Lewes streets, under the control and direction of the "Bonfire Boys" who according to their motto "Are true to each other" and who certainly are true to any pledges they may have given to be of good behaviour, since all mischief to property or person is studiously avoided, and a scene presented year after year as orderly and enjoyable as it is grotesque and fantastic.

[1] "Bonfire in the Past. A retrospect by a Lewes Bonfire Boy" reprinted from the East Sussex News of Nov. 7, 1879, with additions by Mr. William Banks. A valuable contribution to local history, to which the author is much indebted for many of the particulars inserted here.

******

The Gunpowder Plot Conspirators

This shows eight of the thirteen conspirators.
Not shown are Digby, Keyes, Rookwood, Grant and Tresham.

******

The Spirit of the Downs
By Arthur Beckett
(Published London: Methuen & Co., 1909)

Chapter XVIII A SOUTH DOWN SATURNALIA
(pages 204-223)

I

In turning over my collection of Sussex *ana* in the early days of one November I came across the following extract from an old churchwarden's account-book belonging to one of the parishes of Lewes :—

> "1723. Nov. ye 5th. Item: Pd ye Ringers being ye Day of Deliverance from ye powder plot... 2/6."

So, the anniversary of this "Day of Deliverance" being again at hand, I summoned the Companion, and said to him:

"Come, let us go and assist in the worship of Moloch."

"If I am to take part in any mummery," answered the Companion, "I must know first what it means; for if I have prejudices against either Popery or Protestantism I should prefer not to exhibit them in public."

"Chut!" I said. "This celebration, which we are about to witness, was shorn of all real religious significance long ago. Lewes prides itself upon its Protestant feeling, but efforts to invest the saturnalia with a religious association are useless. It is a survival and a revival of those old-time demonstrations against Romanism, which were the excuse for a licence for men to lose their reason during a few short hours in the year. In

Lewes the event is looked upon in the light of a local ritual: former residents return to the town to celebrate it, but all who take part in the affair have the one and only object of a night's amusement, and it would be absurd to consider their excuses. I cannot allow you to miss the celebration; it is one in which Lewes leads England, for no other place approaches it in the splendour of the display. Let us go."

In this manner was the Companion at length reassured. Then, with the old cry of "Io Saturnalia!" we set forth to Lewes to play our part in a celebration which, in Sussex, is, as I shall presently show, no small matter.

Shortly before five o'clock we found ourselves in the principal street of the ancient town, bustling with people, protected by patrols of police, and resounding with the blows of hammers as carpenters boarded up doorways and windows, and covered in area gratings. All business had ceased; the front of both the County Hall and the Town Hall was closely covered with wooden hoardings; the windows of the White Hart Hotel were guarded with wire blinds; while those of shops, public buildings and private houses, were barricaded with deal boards or special shutters, as if for a siege, this precaution being necessary for protection against the Bonfire Boys' inherent practice of throwing fireworks in all directions.

All these things are done because Lewes is the strong citadel of Bonfiredom, for the celebration of "The Fifth" acts like a fever upon the Lewesian, and it is surprising how many sedate inhabitants of this sleepy Sussex town awake from the somnolence of three hundred and sixty-four days to the delights and the revelry of the three hundred and sixty-fifth. To the heart of the Lewes Bonfire Boy, November the fifth is dearest of all the days in the year. He looks upon its saturnalia as an event of national significance—some would say of religious significance as well, and that to him it takes the place of a saint's day in the Papal Calendar.

The hooligan element is in strong force, though the streets are so well policed that, as a rule, the rough confines his antics to the lusty shouting of popular songs, or just sufficient horseplay to mark his character. Still, it is better to carry a stout stick than to go unprotected, for a hard felt hat has a strong attraction for the hooligan. Also, it is well to wear old clothes and to cover the eyes with wire goggles against stray sparks. Thus armed and guarded, we were prepared for the fray.

According to custom, the proceedings open at 5 p.m. with the Bonfire Boys' "prayers" in Commercial Square, a quaint ritual in which all join in intoning a condemnation of Roman Catholicism, and the attempts of Guido Fawkes to blow up the Parliament of King James the First in 1605; but, as the local rhyme says, "By God's providence he was catcht," and his fell design thus frustrated. After the recital of the "prayers" the first procession is formed, for each society has five or six, whose efforts, later in the evening, culminate in a grand display of their united forces.

Then to the tune of the special march, "Bonfire Boys are out To-night," the first procession gets under way. It is brave with banners, bearing such inscriptions as "Our Faith and Freedom we will Maintain," and "May we never engage in a Bad Cause or Flinch in a Good One." For a time the masqueraders march in total darkness, but on reaching the tunnel on the way to the Wallands, a signal is given, torches are suddenly lighted, and the saturnalia is seen emerging into the sylvan scenery of the park, the effect being at once imposing and picturesque.

Each society proceeds independently with its celebration in a similar manner, until the hour arrives at which the "Grand Procession" has been announced to start. The ordering of this, the event of the evening, occupies some considerable time, and while the officers are marshalling their men and distributing fresh torches, the fusillade of fireworks and the shouts of the populace almost drown their words of command.

At length all is in readiness, a sky-rocket gives the signal to start, and at once the whole column bursts into flame.

We find it well to hold on to a wall to avoid being swept away by the great throng of people. At the head of the procession ride twenty "Lady Lancers," followed by the "Commander-in-chief" with a brilliant staff of Bonfire Boys in miscellaneous military uniforms: lancers, dragoons, hussars, horse artillery and mounted rifles. Every kind of costume appears to be represented in the procession, and many of them are really splendid, for the Bonfire Societies offer prizes for the best. Following the first brass band is a line of "ecclesiastics in full canonicals." They support the "Archbishop," who is to deliver a patriotic speech at the fire, and commit the effigies to the flames. These figures include monstrous representations of Guido Fawkes, of infamous memory; one of the pope, an effigy that the Bonfire Boys are careful to declare stands for a system and not for a particular person, and one or more representations of noted criminals of the year. All these effigies are of elaborate workmanship, and manufactured locally, are stuffed with fireworks, and are sometimes made with mechanically moving heads and limbs.

The "Ancient Key of the Borough of Lewes" is carried in front of the Town Society's procession; and at intervals in the long column large firework wheels are lighted, and borne aloft on specially constructed platforms. Then, after many more bands—for the Bonfire Societies are proud of their music — come tableaux, illustrating events of national and topical interest, drawn on trolleys, filled with fireworks, and executed with such expense of money and ingenuity that it seems a pity that they should have to find their fate in the fire. But Moloch refuses nothing that is cast into his maw; and his fanatic priests, the Lewes Bonfire Boys, think nothing is too good for his sacrifice.

The column of masqueraders and spectators flows down the narrow High Street like an unfolding ribbon. Hundreds of torches illuminate it; at intervals big blazing tar-barrels are dragged by iron chains; red and green fire, burnt in long iron ladles, illumines the fantastic faces of the revellers like the witches of a Walpurgis Nacht, and flares in the face of the old houses of the town, where calmer feminine Lewes observes the show from the safety of windows. The saturnalia is no fit spectacle for a woman to witness from any place outside the walls of a house, for every petticoat—and there are not a few—attracts a storm of fiery serpents, and frequently the night is filled with sudden shrieks of frightened females, the victims of unwelcome attention on the part of the firework-throwing Bonfire Boy.

The danger of these detonators may not be despised, for the Lewes celebrant is a master in the making of "chasers" and "rousers." His speciality is the "rouser" of terrifying power—filled with powder from the mills of Battle; and he has a peculiar manner of firing it. He either lights the touch, puts the firework on the ground, and directs its course with a notched stick; or he places four "rousers" together, pointing in various directions, and then firing all at once, spreads consternation everywhere. The thickest crowds receive the largest amount of attention.

Amid the prodigal blaze of Bengal lights the procession reaches the first "funeral" pile in the Square before the County Hall. The bonfires are built in the public streets, and this is one of the biggest. The Square is absolutely impassable, and the air is suffocating with the fumes of sulphur from discharged fireworks. The "Lord Bishop" of the Borough mounts a platform and delivers his oration, hardly a word of which reaches the crowd, so great is the uproar. No one heeds him, for on the morrow all that he says will be read in the local papers, and we shall learn that his address glowed with patriotic feeling and Protestant sentiment, that he condemned the evils of the clay, such as "alcohol," racing and capitalism; congratulated the local mayor on his election to office; that his remarks were full of other topical allusions, and that he concluded by thanking subscribers and press for their support in enabling the Society to carry out the celebration.

Then the Borough Bonfire Boys' effigies are beaten with sticks, the torch is applied to them, and they emit ten thousand sparks from concealed fireworks; a bomb, hidden in each head, blows off that member, the poor remains are cast to the flames, and the fanatics dance round the fire, screaming the bonfire hymn. And when the last effigy has been cremated the procession is reformed and the march is continued to Commercial Square.

The Commercial Square Society is considered the wealthiest brotherhood of Bonfire Boys in Lewes. It is noted for the splendour of its dresses, for the magnificence of its tableaux, and for the profusion of its fireworks, torches and coloured fires. The Society's "grand" procession is marshalled about 10.30 p.m., and, without exaggeration, it may be described as a splendid and imposing pageant. The "obsequies" are under the direction of the "Archbishop" of St John Sub Castro and his staff, and, though similar to those of the Borough Society, owing to the number of set pieces, the fireworks resemble in character those seen at a Brock's benefit. A popular device is the Union Jack; and the "wheels," gerbs and Roman candles would do credit to a Crystal Palace display.

The ceremony of speech-making and cremation proceeds as in the manner of the first fire. So fierce are the flames that some of the spectators place their hats before their faces as a protection against the fiery heat, and the men holding the effigies in front of the fire are preserved from its flames by protecting shields. The pushing of the crowd, confined by the limits of the Square, is not to be denied; women faint in the press; and woe to him who falls!

By the time the fire has died down to a mere glow of embers, the crowd appears to have reached the highest pitch of abandonment, and now lets loose all that remains of its pent-up energy. Several of the most daring men and boys dash through the burning mass, which has become so hot as to drive the spectators back against the walls of the houses. It is now that screeching is loudest; now that the unwary may be hurt. The hissing of fireworks, culminating in alarming detonations, is appalling. People are scattered right and left, or press one another against the walls of the buildings. At every discharge of fireworks the crowd sways in an alarming fashion. It is a wonder no one is crushed to death, for the object of the Lewes Bonfire Boy is to spread confusion, and confusion reigns supreme in the old streets of Lewes for some eight or ten hours.

Then the thousands who have crammed Commercial Square make their way to the suburb of the Cliffe, where—the street being narrow—the crush of people is immense. Here again the ceremony of speeches, and the committing of effigies to the flames is repeated, until the time comes for the procession to proceed to Southover for the last fire of the evening, where the rites are conducted by the "Lord Chancellor of the Manor of Southover," a dignified personage, attired in full judicial robes, who is attended by a page, a trumpeter, mace and sword-bearers, and who dons a black cap before he commits the figures to the flames.

On the stroke of midnight the fire-brigade visits the site of each fire and extinguishes the dying embers by means of the hose. Each Society returns to its own headquarters to conclude its ceremonies with "bonfire prayers" and the singing of the National Anthem. A few minutes later come the Corporation dustmen with their carts, and collect the charcoal and remains of burnt wood. By one o'clock the streets are comparatively quiet, and next morning, with the exception of a rocket case lying here and there, and the blackened patches in the roadway that mark the places where the fires have been, the streets have resumed their normal appearance of old-world sobriety. For the majority the saturnalia exists as a mere memory until another year; it is only the poor unfortunate folk who have more painful reminders of the celebration in the shape of burns and bruises, by whom the event is remembered with regret.

II

On the morrow I observed to the Companion that such a saturnalia as we had witnessed must have a history of no little interest to one who professed to concern himself with the manners and customs of the people. "I am going," I said, "to seek out the oldest Bonfire Boy in Lewes, and ply him with my questions."

"I decline to go with you," declared the Companion; "and I regret that you prevailed upon me to play a part in the licensed riot of last night. I have hitherto regarded myself as a respectable citizen, but during the last few hours I have had to reconsider my claim to that position. I wish you well in your quest, but I will, on no account, either aid or abet you."

So saying, he buried himself in the morning paper, and, for my purpose, I set out to find the oldest Bonfire Boy in Lewes. I discovered him in Mr William Banks of Southover. When I had explained my mission he provided me with a copy of an old pamphlet, from which I have gathered certain of the following particulars.

The annual commemoration of the Gunpowder Plot in Lewes is traced back with certainty for a century and a half, though it is believed that the celebration had its origin at a much earlier date—so far back, indeed, as two centuries ago. It is proved that the carnival had died down before the accession of James the Second, but on its revival during the days of that monarch it became an exceedingly popular event, and the burning of the pope's effigy was a spectacle in which the common people took a peculiar delight. The figures of the pope and Guy Fawkes were elaborately executed in wax, and the former was expensively clothed in a handsome robe and tiara. Seated in a Papal chair this effigy was carried on a car in a procession of persons representing Cardinals and Jesuits. On the car stood a buffoon, disguised as a devil with horns and tail. After perambulating the town the "pope" was presented to the flames, amid the shouts of the populace.

Even in these early days, no expense seems to have been spared in carrying out the carnival; and the procession itself cost no less than £1000.

For reasons not recorded, local interest in the commemoration seems to have subsided until the early years of the nineteenth century, though some sort of celebration was always carried through—chiefly the lighting of huge bonfires built in prominent places. During the first quarter of the century certain Lewesians determined to put new life into the annual demonstration, and the popular event was properly organised. Unfortunately, the revived saturnalia was characterised by the perpetration of acts of incendiarism, and damage to private property; and Lewes brought itself under the notice of the law. In 1829 the custom of dragging flaming tar-barrels through the streets was inaugurated; and the use of such dangerous combustibles as fire-balls became common. The magistrates therefore, by issuing cautions, sought to suppress the proceedings. The Lewes Bonfire Boys merely laughed; and carried out the carnival of the following year with greater energy than ever. In 1832 the town authorities made another attempt to extinguish local enthusiasm in the display, but to no purpose; though no serious disturbance is reported until the year 1838. On that occasion a local magistrate ran foul of a number of Bonfire Boys, who were engaged in burning a tar-barrel on the Cliffe Bridge; and owing to the free use of the bludgeon, made use of by certain roughs, rendered bitter by a feeling against the authorities on account of attempts to suppress their proceedings, several arrests were made by the police, and fines of £15 and under were inflicted upon the most riotous offenders by the bench.

For the next few years the Lewes Bonfire Boys were inclined to carry out their proceedings in a peaceful fashion, though fireworks and blazing tar-barrels in the public streets were still characteristic features of the *fête*. A big bonfire blazed on the Coombe Hill; and peals were rung on the bells of Southover Church. Had they been left to continue these devices the demonstrators might have been satisfied; but in 1841 the police, determined to stop the custom of throwing fire-balls and dragging lighted tar-barrels through the town, swore in a number of special constables to assist the regular force. These plans coming to the ears of the Bonfire Boys, they armed themselves with staves, with the result that several free fights took place, Superintendent Flanigan was knocked down with a boulder beaten with a bludgeon and trampled upon; and many of his men were severely maltreated. At the following assizes some twenty rioters were indicted and sent to prison for terms varying from a fortnight to two months; and at the expiration of their sentences were required to enter into recognisances in sums of £100 and £50 to keep the peace for two years.

The result of this firm action on the part of the police was apparent in the demonstration of the following November. The Bonfire Boys reduced the number of their tar-barrels to two, but compensated themselves for this show of deference to authority by introducing, for the first time, a band of music into the procession.

Having gained even so small a point, the police endeavoured to prevail upon the leaders of the Bonfire movement to give way upon others. Persuasion was directed principally against the holding of the saturnalia in the streets, and other places, less public, but certainly safer, were suggested. The Bonfire Boys promptly declined to listen to the proposal; and on the evening of the 5th of November 1846, some hundreds of men and boys, mostly disguised, and carrying sticks and staves, marched through the town, and then, to the alarm of the more peaceful inhabitants, rushed through the streets at a great pace, dragging flaming tar-barrels in their train. Not satisfied with this, the mob proceeded to the house of Mr Blackman, a local magistrate, piled a number of barrels in front of the building and set them alight, the flames rising to such a height that the inmates were much alarmed. In order to allay the fears of his household Mr Blackman went out, and in a mild but firm manner desired the mob to disperse. But its members, who were in no mood to heed the magistrate's request, received his remarks with a storm of derisive jeers, and aggravated their action by adding fresh fuel to the fire, until the flames flared more fiercely than before. Finding his persuasive efforts futile, Mr Blackman exhibited more courage and determination by attempting to take one of the transgressors into custody, when another of the crowd dealt him a heavy blow over the eye with a bludgeon, and he fell to the ground, apparently lifeless. The magistrate was taken within doors in a condition of insensibility; his recovery being slow and attended with much suffering. In spite of this cowardly act, the demonstrators did not disperse until they had done further damage.

The proceedings of the Bonfire Boys on this occasion inspired "An Old Inhabitant" (said to be the late M.A. Lower) to publish in a pamphlet some "Observations on the Doings in Lewes on the Evening of the Fifth of November 1846, with a few words to parties interested." The pamphlet was an attack on the saturnalia, and an appeal to the inhabitants to discountenance further demonstrations. The writer describes the scene as "a disgusting parade of disguises, bludgeons and riot," distinguished by "the burning of tar-barrels, thirty or upwards in number," and states further that the mob held the streets from six p.m. until the remains of the fire were put out at half-past twelve.

The author of these "Observations" declared that no individual inhabitant of the town dare allow himself to be suspected of being unfavourable to the demonstrators; if so, he was a marked man, liable to personal ill-use and insult, his house was likely to be beset, and tar-barrels burned before it. If a memorial, requesting the magistrates to exercise their powers and prevent a recurrence of the saturnalia, were sent round the town for signatures, it would be found that many of the most respectable inhabitants would decline to sign it, "not they do not feel the impropriety of the proceedings, but from the want of a proper moral courage, and from the fear that their property or premises may be injured by the hand of the malicious villain, or perhaps the midnight incendiary."

"An Old Inhabitant" continues to inveigh against the Bonfire Boys of Lewes, likening them in their love of costume and disguise to assassins, and characterising such disguise as worthy of "the poison-cup and the stiletto of the Italian bravo." Finally, he appeals to the inhabitants to suppress a recurrence of the carnival, and points out its dangers to the interest of local trade, the foolhardiness of letting off fireworks, of blazing tar-barrels, and the burning of a huge bonfire in the street in front of the County Hall, "so that the sparks and flames fly higher than the top of the building, which is the depository of the whole of the County Records, and in which not one room or closet is fire-proof."

Prior to the proceedings of the next commemoration, the magistrates determined to put a stop to the celebration. Among the Bonfire Boys this decision caused considerable consternation. In pursuance of the order of the bench, the police served summonses on the principal tradesmen and other respectable inhabitants; requiring their attendance at the County Hall to be sworn in as special constables. This action was unpopular. A strong disinclination to serve was manifested by many, and a special private meeting of the parties concerned was promptly held at the "Star" Hotel. There the common feeling found voice. A memorial was promoted, suggesting that the means proposed by the magistrates to suppress the celebration were not the best to employ in effecting the desired object, inasmuch as if special constables were commissioned, private interest and sympathy would effectually check any exertion made to apprehend the offenders. Other means, advised the memorialists, should be made use of and the magistrates were requested to withdraw the summonses. A deputation of citizens presented the petition, containing 108 signatures out of a possible 170, to the bench before a crowded court. After listening to the views of the memorialists, the magistrates expressed their inability to accede to the desire of the petitioners; the chairman said that the bench had taken every precaution in their power, and were then in communication with the Secretary of State, with a view to stopping the demonstration; and, with a few exceptions, the whole of the persons summoned were promptly sworn in as special police.

The Bonfire Boys took prompt action. On the night of the 4th November, the special constables held a meeting, and on their way to the place of assembly they were assaulted by bands of defiant Bonfire Boys, who awaited them in different parts of the High Street. The demonstration of the following night promised sport for the rough and the rowdy. In anticipation of this, Lord Chichester and Sir Henry Shiffner, Bart., two members of the bench of magistrates, promptly came into the town. On the same night (the 4th), the demonstrators began their battle against authority by lighting tar-barrels in several byways, and causing disturbances in some of the principal streets. But the police also, had made their plans. Captain Mackay, in command of a large force of constables, had caused a chain to be fastened to the railings on each side of the road near Keere Street, and, with a number of his men, lay ambush in Rotton Row. Nothing of an alarming happened until midnight. Then a blazing tar-barrel was seen coming down St Ann's Hill, drawn by seventy or eighty men, and, on arriving at the chain several of them stumbled and fell. At once the police rushed upon the rioters, a severe scuffle ensued, and after a free fight about a dozen of the ringleaders were secured and led to the cells.

This preliminary skirmish promised much for the morrow. The morning of "The Fifth" saw an excited people in the old streets of Lewes. The Bonfire Boys were set upon resistance; the police expected this and were prepared for it. At mid-day a hundred men of the A Division of the Metropolitan Police came into Lewes, and, at dusk, were formed up in front of the County Hall. The town had been divided into districts, and each district was paraded by a body of "special" constables, armed with staves. As evening approached the streets became more populous, squibs, crackers and other fireworks were discharged with impunity, but beyond watching these proceedings, the police offered no opposition.

Eight o'clock came and the crowd had greatly increased. Presently the mail-gig from Brighton dashed by the County Hall at a furious pace, the horse having been frightened by a firework. All efforts of the driver to stop the animal were unavailing. The gig dashed down the street, and, inclining to the right, came into violent contact with the protruding window of a house at the corner of St

Martin's Lane. The driver was pitched to the ground and picked up insensible; a passing pedestrian was run over and severely bruised. The Bonfire Boys had begun their display in no undecided manner.

The fact was immediately realised by the magistrates, who promptly determined to clear the streets. Mounting the steps of the County Hall, Lord Chichester promptly read the Riot Act, counselled, in his own words, the people to disperse, and gave them five minutes by the clock in which to act upon his advice. Only a few of the more timid attempted to depart, and the five minutes being passed, the police were commanded to charge the multitude. By these means the streets were cleared, but in the mêlée many Metropolitan constables were seriously hurt. On the following morning their departure was attended by a crowd who hooted them heartily and insulted them mercilessly.

Nor did this memorable celebration end here. Some evenings later a number of Bonfire Boys assembled, rolled blazing tar-barrels round the town, and fired squibs and crackers in the High Street, without any interference on the part of the local police, who had been instructed not to interfere. This system of semi-rioting was continued for several evenings, and those persons who had publicly manifested hostility to the proceedings of the Bonfire Boys had the windows of their houses broken.

So much for the proposal of the police to employ force in the suppression of the demonstration. The authorities now realised that they must use other means if they wished to preserve peace. The question of compromise was considered. In the following year two of the leaders of the Bonfire Boys decided to wait upon the magistrates and request them to leave the custody of the town in their hands. The magistrates, very properly, agreed. To promote their plans for the proper conduct of the proceedings, the Bonfire Boys accepted the aid of the constabulary, a proviso being made that no tar-barrels should be burnt, no fire-balls should be thrown, and no persons should be permitted to perambulate the streets in disguise. The head-boroughs and some of the leading inhabitants were called upon to lend their support, and a committee of tradesmen was formed with the idea of considering the question of celebrating the anniversary outside the town. To serve this end Mr John Ellman offered the Bonfire Boys the use of the Wallands Estate. The offer was gratefully accepted, and, in the presence of many thousands of spectators, a splendid display was carried through in a manner satisfactory to all parties. This plan was pursued during many succeeding celebrations, each of which was signally successful and free from the objections which had characterised many earlier carnivals.

About 1850, the pope made a determined attempt to persuade the people of England to his Church. The year is looked upon by the perfervid Lewesian as one of the most important in the annals of local bonfireism. The pope's proceedings led the townspeople to give a willing licence to the Bonfire Boys to use the streets of Lewes for the purpose of giving vent to the full manifestation of that Protestant feeling which, at this date, was always the excuse for the celebration. Two great fires were lighted in the roadway—one in front of the County Hall, one in the main street of the Cliffe, and a third on Cliffe Hill. Rockets and "rousers" were used in great profusion, burning tar-barrels were dragged through the thoroughfares; enthusiasm and excitement prevailed everywhere. At midnight a tar-barrel was set ablaze near the spot where the Marian Papists burnt their Protestant brethren to death. The celebration of 1850 seems to have been taken as a permanent permission to return to the old customs connected with this Sussex saturnalia, for, from that date, the Lewes "Boys" made the public streets the scene of the demonstration.

It was not until 1853 that the Bonfire Boys of Lewes decided to organise themselves for the purpose of marching in procession through the streets. Until that date the demonstration had been due to individual enterprise; but in that year the principal tradesmen of the town formed themselves into associations properly organised and officered. The first societies thus formed were those of the "Town" and the "Cliffe." Each had its captains and lieutenants of the procession, of flags and banners and tar-tubs. At this date the "Guernsey" pattern of dress had become popular, and it was decided that the uniform of the members of the first society of Bonfire Boys should be a blue-and-white striped guernsey, white trousers and a white cap; the officers being distinguished by a red sash. This uniform prevailed for some time, until it was succeeded by the general adoption of fancy dress. The effigies of the '53 procession included, in addition to those of the pope and Guy Fawkes, a bear, representing Russia (for the Crimean War was on the political horizon), and a pig labelled "Peter the Papist," standing for a Sussex newspaper proprietor of the day [1], whose continued articles against the demonstration had rendered him exceedingly unpopular with the Bonfire Boys. *[1. The late Mr P. Bacon of Lewes]*

The co-existence of two societies at first caused considerable jealousy, which was let loose when the rival processionists met on the bridge over the Ouse and came to blows. But in the passage of time the Town and Cliffe Societies became reconciled, with the happy result that both bonfire associations agreed to assist each other in carrying out the celebration. Nevertheless, the old rivalry was marked for many years in the custom (that still obtains) of the Borough Bonfire Boys carrying a blazing tar-barrel to the bridge—the line of demarcation between the Town and the Cliffe—and throwing it over the railings into the river.

The two original societies were so well supported that other brotherhoods of Bonfire Boys were brought into being during succeeding years, including the "Commercial Square" and the "Waterloo." All were financially flourishing, and the spirit of rivalry led each society to endeavour to eclipse the shows of its competitors in point of spectacular effects. Each society confined its preliminary processions to its own part of the town, but though rivals in respect of their early parades, every Lewes Bonfire Boy was alike in the desire to surpass all other towns in the display, and, finally, having formed one grand procession, all the societies perambulated the streets with united forces, the fire of each society being visited in turn for the "obsequies."

Owing to a scourge of typhoid attacking the town in 1874, the High Constable persuaded the Bonfire Societies not to carry out the demonstration on usual date. It was decided, therefore, that the saturnalia should be celebrated on a future occasion (when the devastating fever had subsided) as a "day of rejoicing!" On "The Fifth" therefore, the various; societies formed themselves into bodies of special police; and patrolled the town to prevent sundry persons from discharging fireworks or making other disturbance. The "day of rejoicing" came on the 31st of December, after a fall of snow; and it is stated that the effect of the torches and coloured fires in the white streets and on the buildings was peculiarly weird and picturesque.

The headquarters of the Bonfire Societies are at local hotels; and at the first meeting of members for the year the secretary cries "The books are open," and those present throw coins on to the table, as much as £20 sometimes being thus collected in an evening. The officials are elected; and in Lewes it is considered great honour to hold office in one or other of the societies. Collectors are then appointed to visit the inhabitants, whose response is free and unstinted. To this strong financial support is due the splendour and magnificence of the processions of recent years, the extravagance of the firework displays, and the fact that the societies, when in the height of their prosperity, burnt no less than two hundred tar-barrels, and used no less than from 6000 to 8000 flambeaux to illuminate their processions. The bonfires—each of which is as big as a cottage—are built of great piles of faggots and brush-wood on a foundation of barrels, and covered with a dressing of petroleum.

Such is local enthusiasm for, and pride in the saturnalia, that the event is referred to in many a Protestant pulpit; and an annual thanksgiving address is given in Jireh Chapel on the Sunday preceding the celebration to a crowded congregation of Lewes Bonfire Boys and their friends. I have before me a newspaper report of one such service, in which the remarks of the special preacher were received with frequent applause, and certain of his references to things Papal with laughter.

It is not to be expected that this annual feast of the fire-worshippers of Lewes should pass off without accident. Burns and bruises have been common enough, and misfortunes of a more severe character have occasionally occurred. On at least two occasions, a prominent Lewesian lost an eye; in another year a shed used as a store for torches provided a splendid premature blaze.

A big fire in the town in 1904, about a month before "The Fifth," caused the possible dangers attending the celebration to be pressed forcibly upon the inhabitants, and, in consequence, the use of the famous Lewes "rouser" was prohibited.

Recollections of Lewes Bonfiredom call up the names of not a few curious characters, who have been connected with the annual commemoration. Among them was "Old Betty," the sextoness of Southover Cemetery, who, with a short pipe in her mouth, and bearing her distinguishing label of "Tubs, No. 9," walked in the procession dragging a flaming tar-barrel by an iron chain. There is an old Bonfire Boy, a late "Lord Bishop of Lewes," who boasts with pride of preaching the annual carnival "sermon" at the Borough fire for thirty-three years, and who, although he made a target for the fireworks of the mob, while delivering his address from the steps of the County Hall, was never once burnt, in spite of the fact that, on one occasion, a rough endeavoured to burn him with a Roman candle, but who, in consequence, had his fingers broken by the cudgel of some person standing by.

The carnival celebration has, of course, found many detractors who, apart from the religious significance which certain people pretend to attach to it, condemn the celebration on the grounds that it offers to the mob openings for incidents of vulgarity and impropriety. The fact of so many thousands of people, they say, being allowed to roam the streets in all manner of guise, tends to foster acts of a more or less licentious. But it is well to remember that the are so well patrolled by the police, and that even quietest back lanes are so thoroughly public on occasion, that it is almost an impossibility for improper incidents to escape detection, and beyond a few isolated acts of violence and of horse-play carried beyond bounds of reason, the police and public have no really serious complaint to make. In fact, the management of the crowds is so well carried out that thousands persons, including large numbers who have come into the town by special trains, are kept under reasonable control by the local police, strengthened by a large posse—usually a hundred constables—from Brighton. Early in the afternoon people begin to pour into the town from all points of the compass, coming in by train and all kinds of conveyance. The capacity of the local stabling is greatly taxed; and some of the inns and hotels are quite unable to accommodate all the customers seeking refreshment, who, in many instances, secure their drink only after a struggle at the bar counters, and carry it outside to consume in the street.

To the man unacquainted with Lewes, the spectacle of a sleepy town run mad on one evening of the year is for marvel. But, although public opinion have set against the old manner of celebration, and the authorities have somewhat curtailed the liberty Bonfire Boys during recent years, Lewesians may be allowed the credit of keeping up an old and time-honoured folk-custom. The old county town set an example in the celebration that was followed largely by its neighbours; in Eastbourne the annual event was considered of such importance that special editions of the local papers succeeded the evening of the carnival, in which many pages were devoted to a description of the event and the report of the speeches. But so far as other Sussex towns are concerned, the custom is dead; Lewes alone possesses an undying, if diminished, enthusiasm for the celebration of the saturnalia.

******

Mr. Sydney Albert (Bert) Munt 1901-1958

Bert Munt was born in 1901 in the village of Kingston near Lewes, Sussex. As a pre-war Territorial he saw active service in France and Belgium almost from the beginning of the Second World War. He was evacuated, a badly wounded man who had his leg amputated, from Dunkirk in 1940. He was subsequently invalided out of the army.

He returned to his pre-war work at Eastwoods (Lewes) Cement Ltd., he completed 21 years service with the company until failing health in 1958 incapacitated him.

At some stage he moved to 3 Keere Street, Lewes with his wife Doris. Bert was a man of many interests and had several hobbies. His main interest was the town of Lewes and of course Lewes bonfire. He was a member of the Friends of Lewes Society, number 8 Cine Circle and number 1 Tape Circle.

He was secretary of the Lewes Borough Bonfire Society for some years, and as Captain of Tableaux was responsible for designing and helping to make many of their set pieces. He was made the societies first life member, and was until his death Honorary Secretary of the Lewes Bonfire Council.

Bert died on Tuesday 25 November 1958 at Lewes Victoria Hospital; he left a widow, while his parents, both over 80, and were living at 28 Keere Street, Lewes. He also left a sister, Dorothy Philips who lived in Canada, a brother Ron who lived at Iford and another sister, Mrs. M. Davis of Brighton. The funeral was held on 28 November at Westgate Chapel, Lewes followed by internment at the Borough Cemetery.

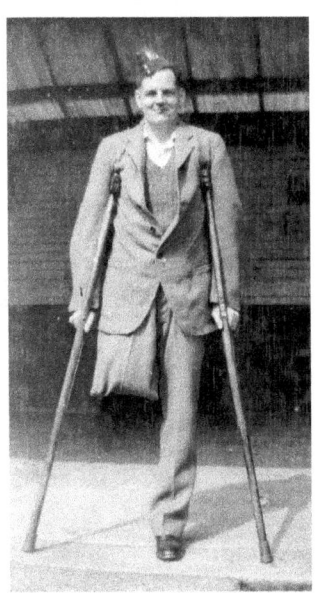

Sydney Albert (Bert) Munt
(Courtesy of Christine Munt)

Bill Munt (father of Bert) carrying tar barrel for Borough
(Courtesy of David Philips)

"BONFIRE"
By
Bert Munt (1958)

"The celebration of the Gunpowder Plot of November 5th, 1605, in Lewes, has persisted so long that it deserves to rank among the historic features of the county town."
Sussex County Magazine, November 1928.

Although thirty years have passed since Arthur Beckett wrote the above, not only does the commemoration still persist, but last year it attracted, among others, the attention of the B.B.C., B.E.A., C.B.S. News and was discussed at some length in a recording made for transmission in Canada. Quite an impressive list for a celebration which has no official support or financial backing from town or county authorities. In years gone by the cost of the celebration would have been almost covered by public subscriptions. With to-day's costs at least four times as high, bonfire societies are now faced with the task of raising the greater part themselves. This they do by organising dances, whist drives, fetes, jumble sales etc., throughout the year.

For at least two months prior to the "Fifth", the work of preparation occupies most of the spare time of the bonfire boys and girls. Each society makes up to four thousand torches and these are made with tow which is wound on to the end of a stick about two feet long and fastened with wire. When soaked in paraffin they give excellent light, very little smoke and burn for about twenty minutes, a time which has been found to be the most suitable.

The societies purchase the fireworks but leave the making of the effigies, tableaux and set-pieces to their own experts. So skilled in the pyrotechnic art have some of these become, that it is difficult to convince the spectator that such elaborate tableaux etc. have indeed been made by amateurs.

One hundred and one other jobs have to be done including making and renovating fancy dresses. These, in the troublesome times prior to the formation of bonfire societies, were probably more useful as disguise. The pioneers, who march at the head of the processions, all wear similar dresses and this custom dates back over one hundred years. The first uniform consisted of a blue and white striped guernsey, white trousers and a woollen cap; the officers being distinguished by a red sash. Over the years the bonfire boys must have rung the changes on almost every kind of costume. In more recent times, however, there has been less change.

Instead, the dresses become more elaborate as the years go by. In this way the Commercial Square Society has built up a collection of Red Indian dresses which never fail to win enthusiastic applause wherever they, are displayed. The Zulu Chiefs of the Borough Society are equally impressive and, like the Vikings of Cliffe, the Rahjas and Rahnees of Southover and the Valencians of South Street, seem to have become almost traditional.

Major societies have in attendance at least two bands and (by a reciprocal arrangement) their ranks are swelled by one or more societies from neighbouring towns and villages. Thus, in the light of hundreds of torches the spectator is presented with a bewildering array of colourful costume.

The high spot comes when four societies unite in one grand procession. Starting at the foot of the downs in the west this procession winds its way through the town descending, as it does so to the level of the river Ouse, once the town's eastern boundary. Here, while the others break away and return to their own areas, the Borough Society march on to the bridge where the customary blazing tar-barrel is hurled into the river.

Each society's own grand procession terminates at its fire. Here, following an address by the appropriate official, the effigies ignite into a fountain of brilliant sparks and balls of coloured fire and, when finally blown to pieces, the reports can be heard for miles. Then follows the igniting of the various tableaux and set-pieces which last year included two "sputniks" one of them complete with dog.

After the fires the thousands of visitors begin to depart but the celebration is not yet over. Each society stages one or more precessions and then terminate their proceedings at the site of the original fires, when these were pitched in the streets. After a short speech by the Commander-in-Chief, the bonfire prayers are recited and Auld Lang Syne and the National Anthem sung.

So ends yet another commemoration of the discovery of the Gunpowder Plot. Much remains to be done, however, and "Bonfire", if it can be said to end at all, will not be over until after the annual dinners. Of all the questions asked on the subject of bonfire the most difficult to answer is, why has it persisted so long? Contemporary writers of magazines and newspaper articles get over the difficulty by linking the celebration with the seventeen protestant martyrs who were burnt at Lewes in the sixteenth century. It is true that the martyrs have a place in bonfire history, but the notion, as one writer put it; "that it was this indelible experience in the town's history that caused the extraordinary zeal", just cannot be substantiated.

As far as the town's history is concerned, Lewesians have far more reason for remembering the destruction of the Priory of St. Pancras. Whatever may have been the justification for turning out the monks the destruction of this noble edifice was an act of sheer vindictive spite. An act which not only robbed Lewes of much of its importance but of a monument which to-day would be attracting thousands of visitors to the town.

These acts of protestant and catholic intolerance, however, took place long before the Gunpowder Plot where bonfire history rightly begins.

"The oldest bonfire society in the world!"

"Fire on Cliffe Hill in 1606"

"It can be taken as an established fact that when the news of the frustration of the plot came to Bridgwater, probably late in the afternoon of the 5th, the townspeople rejoiced and during the evening lit bonfires, and there may have been processions in and around the borough."

Such claims are, of course, not worth consideration for while Guy Fawkes was being questioned and tortured in the Tower, the government of James the First, understandably anxious to exploit the plot's anti-catholic propaganda value to the full, ordered that November 5th should be observed as a holiday for ever. A special service was prepared and there can be little doubt that before the fun and games those early celebrants had first to give thanks for the merciful deliverance of their King.

It is the bonfires that pose intriguing questions. Were they a spontaneous expression of joy? Or were they, as Laurance Whistler suggests, a continuation or revival of the fires of Hallowe'en? Certainly neither church nor government would have objected to the pagan fires becoming anti-papal, and may even have encouraged it.

Whatever the answer, the bonfire was certainly customary and not only has it remained so but the name "Bonfire" has come to mean the whole business of preparing and carrying out a celebration in which the "fire" plays a very small part. The act of taking part is "bonfiring".

While the Lewes bonfire boys can rightly lay claim to fame in this persistence and determination with which they have kept the celebrations going, they can only be traced back, with certainty, for a little over a century and a half.

The excitement, which may have died down, flared up again after the Restoration. In the reign of Charles the Second, popish plots were being manufactured out of thin air. Titus Oates was responsible for the execution of eighteen Roman Catholics, and even the famous diarist, Samuel Pepys, was thrown in gaol on the charge of being one. This too was the hey-day of the Green Ribbon Club who, with their rumour mongers and bonfire pageantries, controlled the London mob. Their great pope-burning orgies were held on November 17th, the anniversary of Elizabeth's accession day when the mob, 100,000 strong, marched behind a dummy pope which they burnt at Smithfield with live cats in his belly to make bin squall realistically. "The men of the Green Ribbon Club may not have been squeamish", writes Arthur Bryant, "but they knew their London Mob."

Had James the Second been content to alleviate the lot of his fellow Roman Catholics, the English people (such was their loyalty and respect for the throne) might well have tolerated him. His measures, however, were far too harsh, even for those days. There was the savage treatment of the poor peasants who had joined in the Monmouth Rebellion and, most important of then all to bonfire boys, his edict, forbidding the customary bonfires on Guy Fawkes Day. This edict probably did more to eliminate the loyalty of subjects than all his other measures put together. Hang us by the score if you must, take our bonfires away, NEVER.

With James deposed, the Dutch Prince, William of Orange on the English Throne and Protestantism once more firmly established, fears of popish plots subsided, and so, with much of the incentive gone, it may be that in many parts of the country interest in Guy Fawkes Day began to fade.

We have evidence, however, that Ye Day of Deliverance from Ye Powder Plot was observed in Lewes in 1723 and again in 1795.

The diary of the late John Holman, High Constable of Lewes, shows that on the night of November 5th, 1813, the "Boys" had a fire on Gallows Bank. This may have been the resumption of the celebration after the Napoleonic wars. It has been suggested too, that the original "bonfire boys", were the men who kept watch by the beacon fires which were built to give warning of the expected invasion.

The celebration of 1829, saw blazing tar barrels being dragged through the streets. The use of fireballs had become common and in an effort to stop these dangerous practices the magistrates issued cautions.

In 1832, an attempt was made to stop the celebration but without success.

In 1838 great rioting occurred and several arrests were made and fines up to £15 imposed. A local magistrate had an encounter with the boys on the bridge over the river Ouse. According to the story handed down, the "Boys" were burning a tar-barrel when the magistrate tried to interfere. The boys grabbed him and lifted him over the railings of the bridge. There he was held until he promised not to interfere again. According to old "Borough" programmes, it was to commemorate this incident that the bonfire boys began the custom (that still obtains) of throwing a blazing tar-barrel into the river. One wonders, however, whether this was not already a long established custom. The barrel is always thrown over on the seaward side and according to Mr Frank R. Williams, a well known Seaford historian, the custom compares with the setting of an old boat on fire, as at Rye on the Sussex coast and letting it drift out to sea. "Those customs", says Mr Williams, "were old pagan rituals and, like the fires, did not suddenly spring up after the attempt by Fawkes to blow up parliament."

Special Constables were sworn in for another attempt to stop the celebration in 1841. The bonfire boys armed themselves and Superintendent Flanigan and some of his men were roughly treated. At the following Assizes over twenty of the rioters were sent to prison for terms of up to two months.

The following year the proceedings were more orderly. The bonfire boys reduced the number of tar-barrels but compensated themselves by introducing a band of music for the first time.

In 1846, the police again tried to stop the celebration. This led to core rioting and another magistrate was seriously injured. A pamphlet was published by "An Old

Inhabitant" entitled, "Observations on the Doings in Lewes on the Evening of the Fifth of November, 1846." This attack on the bonfire boys, described the scene as, "a disgusting parade of disguises, bludgeons and riot, distinguished by the burning of tar-barrels, thirty or upwards in number. The mob held the streets from 6pm until the remains of fire were put out at half-past 12." For their love of costume and disguise, he likened the bonfire boys to assassins, and pointed out the foolhardiness of letting off fireworks, of blazing tar-barrels and the burning of a huge bonfire in front of the County Hall, "so that the sparks and flames fly higher than the top of the building, which is the depository of the County Records, and in which not one room or closet is fireproof."

The climax was reached in 1847 when, in a determined effort to stop the celebration, 170 of the principal tradesmen and "other respectable inhabitants" were summoned to be sworn in as Special Constables. Many of these were very reluctant to serve and not without reason for, on their way to a meeting on the night of November 4th, they were attached by bonfire boys in the High Street. "The demonstration of the following night", wrote Arthur Beckett, "promised sport for the rough and the rowdy."

In anticipation of this, Lord Chichester and Sir Henry Shiffner, Bart., two members of the bench of magistrates, promptly came into the town. On the same night (the 4th), the demonstrators began their battle with authority by lighting tar-barrels in several byways and causing disturbances in some of the principal streets. But the police had also made their plans. Captain Mackay, in command of a large force of constables, had caused a chain to be fastened to the railings on each side of the road near Keere Street and, with a number of his men, lay in ambush in Rotten How. Nothing of an alarming character happened until midnight. Then a blazing tar-barrel was seen coming down St. Anne's Hill, drawn by some seventy or eighty men and, on arriving at the chain, several of them stumbled and fell. At once the police rushed upon the rioters, a severe scuffle ensued and, after a free fight, about a dozen of the ringleaders were secured and led to the cells.

This preliminary skirmish promised much for the morrow. The morning of the "The Fifth" saw an excited people in the streets of Lewes. The Bonfire Boys were set upon resistance; the police expected this and were prepares for it. At mid-day a. hundred men of the A Division of the Metropolitan Police came into Lewes and, at dusk, were formed up in front of the County Hall. The town had been divided into districts and each district was paraded by a body of special constables, armed with staves. As evening approached the streets became more populous; squibs, crackers and other fireworks were discharged with impunity but, beyond watching these proceedings, the police offered no opposition.

Eight o'clock came and the crowd had greatly increased. Presently the mail-gig from Brighton dashed down the High Street at a furious pace, the horse having been frightened by fireworks. The gig came into contact with the protruding window of a house at the corner of St. Martin's Lane. The driver was picked up insensible; a passing pedestrian was run over and severely bruised. The Bonfire Boys had begun their display in no uncertain manner.

This fact was immediately realised by the magistrates, who promptly determined to clear the streets. Mounting the steps of the County Hall, Lord Chichester read the Riot Act, counselled in his own words the people to disperse and gave them five minutes by the clock in which to act upon his advice. Only a few of the more timid attempted to depart and, the five minutes being passed, the police were commanded to charge the multitude. By these means the streets were cleared but, in the melee, many Metropolitan constables were seriously hurt. On the following morning their departure was attended by a crowd who hooted them heartily and insulted them mercilessly.

Nor did this memorable celebration end here. Some evenings later a number of Bonfire Boys assembled, rolled blazing tar-barrels round the town and fired squibs and crackers in the High Street, without any interference on the part of the local police who had been instructed not to interfere. This system of semi-rioting was continued for several evenings and those persons who had publicly manifested hostility to the proceedings of the Bonfire Boys had the windows of their houses broken.

But why all this riotous behaviour? A reason is not hard to find, as these quotes from a document presented by demonstrating labourers of the neighbouring village of Ringmer and reported in the "Times" of November 25th 1830, show ".....and we ask whether 7d. a day is sufficient for a working man to keep up the strength necessary to the execution of the labour he has to do......Have we no right to complain that we have been obliged for so long a period to go to our daily toil with only potatoes in our satchels.....and on returning to our cottages to be welcomed by the meagre and half famished offspring of our toil worn bodies? We therefore ask for married men 2s. 6d. a day in summer and 2s. 3d. a day in winter."

In "Magnificent Journey", Francis Williams says that, "this revolt, as it was called, spread in some measure across the whole of Southern England. Commissions were appointed and, by the time their work was finished, of the labourers who had dared speak out against their masters and ask for more than 7d. a day, 9 had been hanged, 459 transported for life and 400 imprisoned with hard labour." Small wonder that feelings ran high on bonfire night.

"Although," said "The Express Herald", "apparently the law had gained the best of the day, it was realised that persuasion was better than force, and before the "The Fifth" in the year 1848, it was decided to form a committee local tradesmen, with the late Mr B. Flint as Chairman, to make the arrangements." This apparently proved very successful and it is recorded that the celebration this year," was the most orderly in memory". The newspaper report also stated that, "The Town Band headed the procession which formed up outside the White Hart and, together with about 2,000 spectators, wended its way to the Wallands."

Celebrating the anniversary outside the town was made possible by Mr John Ellman whose offer of the use of the Wallands Estate was gratefully accepted by the Bonfire Boys.

The Bonfire Boys, in order to secure the co-operation of the authorities, had to agree to their proviso that no tar-barrels should be burnt, no fire-balls thrown and no person permitted to adopt disguise and, although the same procedure was adopted the following year, it must have seemed very tame to the Bonfire Boys. So tame, in fact, that they must soon have lost interest and those on the Wallands Estate been the last of the Lewes celebrations. But in 1829, while the Bonfire Boys were more concerned with empty bellys, Roman Catholic emancipation had begun. By 1838, "The Times" was observing that the celebrations at Lewes and other Sussex towns, had now grown foreign to the enlightened feeling and spirit of the times.

But when, twelve years later, Pope Pius the Ninth issued a bull re-establishing a Roman Catholic Hierarcy in England, "The Times" led the press in condemning "Papal aggression". The indignation in every part of the country that no fewer than 6,700 addresses to Her Majesty the Queen, calling upon her and the government to resist the usurpation, had been voted by the end of the year.

In his book, "A Hundred Years of Catholic Emancipation" Denis Gwynn says; "Not for years had there been such a coincidence of popular excitement with the festivities of Guy Fawkes' Day. Lord John Russell's letter, appearing on 4th November, gave the signal for a gorgeous display of bonfires, in which effigies of Cardinal Wiseman and of the Pope provided an element of real excitement and patriotic indignation. At Salisbury a complete outfit of effigies of the Pope, Wiseman and the twelve new Catholic bishops had been elaborately staged. By five o'clock in the afternoon the main streets had become impassable with a dense and excited crowd. At dusk some hundreds of torches were lit in preparation for the grand spectacle at half-past six, when "his Holiness was brought out" (to quote the newspaper report) "amid the cheering of the populace. The procession being formed, proceeded in the following order; torch-bearers, brass-band, torch-bearers, his Holiness in full pontificals, seated in a huge chair; torch-bearers, bishops, three abreast; torch-bearers, Cardinal Wiseman, etc. etc. Within the precincts of the close the National Anthem was played amid deafening cheers. The procession having paraded the duty, the effigies were taken to Green Croft, where, over a large number of faggots end barrels of tar, a huge platform was erected of timber; the effigies were placed thereon, and a volley of rockets sent up. The band played the Doxology, and deafening cheers followed. A light being supplied to the combustibles below, the flames rose to the platform; hundreds of fireworks were then hurled at the effigies. Then followed the Morning Hymn and the National Anthem, in which thousands joined."

The "Sussex Weekly Advertiser" said that, "at Eastbourne the celebration was invested with an unusual degree of interest as being the popular mode of manifesting disapprobation of the late aggressive measures of Rome". So great was the indignation, here at Lewes, that the townspeople, who only three years before had enlisted the aid of a hundred Metropolitan police to get them off them, "now gave", says Arthur Beckett, "a willing licence to the Bonfire Boys to use the streets of Lewes for the purpose of giving vent to the full manifestation of the protestant feeling."

Although the "Sussex Weekly Advertiser" reported only the dragging of tar-barrels down St. Anne's Hill, fireworks in plenty and a fire in front of the County Hall, in the annals of Lewes bonfire the date 1850 rates second only in importance to 1605.

Of the night of November 5th 1851, the "Sussex Weekly Advertiser" says; "The streets of Lewes were, alas, a scene of uninterrupted disorder. There were some demonstrations in Cliffe but towards 9 o'clock they were concluded. There was, consequently, a general union of forces in the High Street." Describing what it called the disgraceful proceedings, the paper said; "King Mob had it all his own way", and added, "the mere mob did not provide the funds which were wasted on the fifth. They must have come from higher sources and, so long as such is the case, it is folly to expect that the blot which is annually cast on the good sense and respectability of the inhabitants of Lewes can be wiped away."

The paper's Editor, Peter Bacon, was obviously not in favour of the celebrations and the Bonfire Boys were not long in noting the fact. In its report of the celebration of 1852, the paper says; "The Sussex Weekly Advertiser has so often reported the disgraceful proceedings and this event was no exception. There was a continuous discharge of fireworks in front of the County Hall and effigies of Guy Fawkes, the Pope or Cardinal Wiseman, and the Editor of this newspaper in the shape of a pig were burnt." Inspite of this, the paper said, it would still go on protesting and in 1853 it still was.

"This year", it said, "there were more than usually intensive preparations", and added; "We understand that very considerable sums were subscribed for this celebration and a committee was formed to obtain donations and arrange proceedings. One tradesman is said to have contributed £20 and another £10, while some of our most respectable inhabitants are reported to have openly sanctioned the proceedings both in purse and in person."

Although it is obvious that some sort of an organisation had existed since 1843, the Lewes Bonfire Society, now the Lewes "Borough" Bonfire Society, take this as being the year of their formation and the fact that the Bonfire Boys had now become properly officered and organised for the purpose of marching in procession through the streets of Lewes seems to have caused Peter Bacon to have given up the struggle. "The Sussex Weekly Advertiser" makes no further mention of the celebrations for several years but by 1859 we know from early programmes, that encouraged by the success of the first, two more societies had been formed. One in what was then the neighbouring village of Cliffe, and a second Lewes society, Commercial Square. In all of them and this applies to societies that were formed in other Sussex towns, "No Popery" became the keynote of the celebration and Pope Pius the Ninth, the new arch villain of the piece.

The "Church Times" of July 22nd 1955 in reporting the centenary of the Society of St. Margaret, gave us a glimpse of the bitterness that prevailed at that time. Here is a quote from the report.

"But the heroic nature of their work and the obvious dedication of their lives did nothing to soften the hearts of their scornful opponents. In November 1857, occurred the brutal affair of the Lewes riot. At the funeral of the first Sister who died, Novice Amy, a furious mob assaulted the Sisters in the Churchyard at Lewes. The Sisters with Dr Neale were actually rescued by the police."

In 1859, the service of thanksgiving, prepared in 1605, was deleted from the English prayer book and, the violent outburst against the re-establishment of the Roman Catholic Church in England having failed in its purpose, it was natural that with the passing of the years much of the excitement died down.

While, it is true, they continued to burn an effigy of "the" pope and their bishops to deliver anti-catholic speeches, the tableaux and banners began to take note of other happenings. Garibaldi was honoured, the Russians, Turks and Japanese condemned or honoured according to current feelings. In fact, as one writer says; "through the years, bonfire tableaux have reflected the changing hatreds of the English people".

And so, except for an outbreak of typhoid fever, which caused the celebration of 1874 to be postponed until December 31st and the formation of other Lewes societies, the celebrations pursued an uneventful course until 1904. In that year fireworks in the streets were banned and, although in 1905 the Bonfire Boys acted up to their undertaking to have smaller fires, in 1906 these too were banned. This set-back hit the Bonfire Boys hard and, for a year or two, until sites for the fires could be found on the outskirts of the town, two societies ceased to function and two more where forced to amalgamate.

It is generally believed that it was a big fire in the High Street which led to the banning of the fireworks and the fires but the reports of the 1906 celebration prove that there was very much more reason than that. So nearly, in fact, was this the end of Lewes bonfire that one local paper began its report like this; "Bonfire is Dead: Long live the memory of the glorious "Fifths" that have been." The same paper goes on to refer to, "the Russian-like methods of those who saw fit to pack the town with hired policemen. The only wonder", it added, "was a squadron of cavalry with loaded rifles in readiness to quell any disturbance."

Addressing the crowd at the Commercial Square and Borough Society's fire which was pitched in a field just beyond the prison, the bishop said; "I need hardly remind you that just previous to last year's celebration the county police authorities issued orders which, had they been enforced, would have prevented the proceedings being carried out in the usual way but as the preparations were far advanced the matter was allowed to remain in abeyance. Perhaps it is not so well known, however, that such orders were the outcome of a petition signed, it is believed, by not more than 100 persons, of whom some, it is also believed, were not residents of Lewes. Such a petition could not claim to represent the feeling of the town and, while many of the signatories were no doubt genuinely apprehensive of injury to person and property (the risk of which was perhaps much magnified) yet the notoriously extreme views of those who engineered the petition would warrant us looking much deeper for the true motives underlying this opposition."

As a "young lady of Brighton", in a letter to the press, lamented; "With no Lewes Rousers, no lighted tar-barrels and no fires to light up the dull old town, the celebration of 1906 was enough to make departed bonfire boys turn in their graves."

According to one estimate, 130 policemen were on duty but so orderly were the proceedings during the evening that only 14 people were arrested for discharging fireworks. The trouble the police had apparently been hoping for came when the Commercial Square and Borough Society's last procession ended. Torches were thrown down on the road and this the police interpreted as an attempt to make a bonfire. During the ensuing disturbance, four bonfire boys were arrested. All of them, William Thomas Gearing, Thomas Ernest Gearing, Eli Dawe and Harold Weston were duly summoned to appear before the magistrates on a charge of having; "unlawfully assembled to disturb the public peace and to cause alarm and then did make a great disturbance to the terror and alarm of His Majesty's subjects there being and against the Peace of our Sovereign Lord the King his Crown and Dignity."

The Court was packed with sympathisers and at the hearing, which was twice adjourned, a great deal of conflicting evidence was heard. The police claimed that the whole affair had been planned and that a roll on a drum was the signal for the torches to be thrown down. The drummer, the late Mr. W. Huggett, however, stoutly maintained that his roll on the drum was the signal for the band to play the National Anthem and so the case against the four bonfire boys collapsed.

At this time too, the illegal manufacture of the famous "Lewes Rouser" was so extensive that many houses, including those of one or two very prominent residents, were being searched by the police. Not altogether successfully, it seems, for one batch they failed to find lay under the flour in the bread trough of a bakehouse on Keere Street.

"The English Churchman and St. James Chronicle" says that it was a Roman Catholic police official who organised this unsuccessful attempt to end the celebrations and this prompts the question why, after all the excitement of 1850 had died down, such an individual should have wanted to end them. A possible explanation is that, towards the end of the nineteenth century, the influence of a very much younger organisation was already changing the character of the celebration. In 1901, in the face of great local opposition, it is said, the memorial to the martyrs who were burnt at Lewes was erected on Cliffe Hill. Thus inspired, the bonfire bishops, who were already coupling the Landing of William Prince of Orange, in 1688 with the Discovery of the Gunpowder Plot, were soon also recalling the grisly catholic fires of the past and by 1905 the Borough Society was parading with a huge banner depicting the martyrs being burnt at the stake and a new "NO POPERY" banner presented by the Loyal Orange Lodge.

Whether this alliance with the Orangemen could be taken

as a good and sufficient reason for a Roman Catholic police official to try and stop the celebration or not, the fact remains that it was during this period of their history, that bonfire boys first commemorated the landing of William, Prince of Orange and honoured the Martyrs, as it was called. Another innovation of the period (probably due to the same influence) was the substitution of an effigy of the pope of the time of the plot, Paul the Fifth, for that of "The Pope".

By 1909 the Borough and Commercial Square Societies were again celebrating on their own and, after the First World War, as well as the three major societies, those of Southover and St. Annes were re-formed and a new society organised in South Street. Influenced at first by D.O.R.A., but afterwards, when the act was repealed, as a matter of free choice, all but one of the Lewes societies seem to have decided that anti-catholic demonstrations were no longer desirable. While, of course, it must always remain a protestant one, the basis of the celebration became the true carnival spirit in which everybody could join.

The martyrs were again brought to the fore in 1949, when Lewes Town Council gave permission for a memorial plaque to be placed on the wall of the Town Hall. In its report of that year's celebration, the "Express Herald", under the sub-heading "Cliffe Pay Tribute to the Martyrs", had this to say; "An innovation in the Cliffe Society's celebration was a tribute paid to the Sussex Martyrs at a plaque which was placed on the wall of the Town Hall early this year. The society included in one of their processions, a replica of the martyrs' memorial which is on the downs above the Cliffe. They halted with it at the plaque and there, with the replica outlined in fire, they remembered those who suffered death for the protestant faith. So was, though only by Cliffe, history repeated and a romantic notion revived.

Few Lewesians, least of all those of the catholic faith, take the Cliffe Society's celebration very seriously. It is, perhaps, a matter of some regret that the publicity given it does occasionally give rise to unfavourable comments on our town and the celebrations as a whole, but the best answer to such critics is contained in an eye-witness account of the celebration of 1953, published in the Catholic newspaper, "Universe".

"I was glad to have seen the celebrations. They corrected my idea of Lewes. I had thought of it as a town which annually disgraced itself with a crude display of bigotry. But bigotry I found only in the town's east end – certainly crude, very silly, laughable in its linking of the day through the co-operation of the Loyal Orange Lodge, with the landing of William of Orange in 1688. I came away from Lewes with a different view of the town as a whole. My memory is principally of carnival, of processions up and down the hills, with thousands of torches, plenty of fireworks, and an extraordinary range of colourful costumes. Most thoroughly I enjoyed it as did 25,000 others."

There are those who mourn the glories of the past but, though tar-barrels, fire-balls and the genuine Lewes Rouser have vanished, the celebrations to-day are more spectacular than ever they have been. Co-operation is the keynote of relations with the authorities and, though their celebrations are of necessity a compromise, to-day's bonfire boys, like their fore-fathers, are still proving their adherence to the Sussex motto; "We wunt be druv."

******

Bonfires in Lewes
A History of the Celebrations on November the Fifth
By
Simon O'Halloran
Published October 1967

Introduction

> Now boys with squibs and crackers play
> And bonfires' blaze turns night to day.
> "Poor Robin's Almanack" 1677.

Each year on the evening of November 5th there is held an elaborate procession through the streets of Lewes, in Sussex. The procession consists of a few hundred men, women and children who are dressed in fancy costume and carry burning torches. Some carry the banners of their own bonfire societies, and a few carry placards with anti-Catholic slogans. The whole procession is organised by the various bonfire societies, which join together to form the Lewes Bonfire Council. After the procession the societies disperse to their own bonfires. The spectacle is one of brilliant colours and loud noises, and the event must be one of the few remaining displays of a folk culture in England.

Ostensibly the event commemorates the successful discovery of the Gunpowder Plot in 1605, in which Guy Fawkes and his fellow conspirators intended to blow up King James I and his Parliament. But whilst this event is commemorated by children and adults in back gardens all over England there is in Lewes an aspect to the celebrations which has brought them notoriety and ensured a spirited continuity over the years.

The original anti-Catholic element in all Fifth of

November celebrations was re-inforced at Lewes, because the town was the scene of the martyrdom at the stake of seventeen Protestants during the Marian Persecutions of the sixteenth century. And so the anti-Catholic element remained in the Lewes celebrations after it had died away almost everywhere else in England. Today one of the bonfire societies still carries "No Popery" banners, but this slogan can have little meaning for casual onlookers, and it remains merely as a quaint reminder of less tolerant days.

Lewes Bonfire Night is now an annual carnival, a treat for the children. Its origins are obscure, and were probably an amalgam of various interests and attitudes during the centuries since 5th November, 1605.

CHAPTER 1

> Moreover, to light a fire is the instinctive and resistant act of man when, at the winter ingress, the curfew is sounded throughout Nature. It indicates a spontaneous, Promethan rebelliousness against the fiat that this recurrent season shall bring foul times, cold darkness, misery and death. Black chaos comes and the fettered gods of the earth say, Let there be light.
> "Return of the Native". Thomas Hardy.

The making of fire to celebrate important events is of early significance in the development of man. In Europe generally heathen fire-festivals were held at the time of the Summer and Winter Solstices. In the Christian era the Celtic year was divided by the beginning of Summer (Beltane) and of Winter (Allhallow Even or Hallowe'en which was the day before All Saints' or Allhallows' Day). In his extensive study in anthropology 'The Golden

Bough' Sir James Frazer states: "The first of November marks the turning points of the year in Europe; the one ushers in the genial heat and the rich vegetation of summer, the other heralds, if it does not share, the cold and barrenness of winter." [1] We may conjecture that everywhere throughout Europe the celestial division of the year according to solstices was preceded by what we may call terrestial division of the year according to the beginning of summer and the beginning of winter.

In the Celtic world November 1st. saw the beginning of a new year, when the cattle were brought back from the pastures to the stalls and Samhain (i.e. Summer's end) rites were held to counteract the blight of winter with its fears and dangers for man and beast alike. "In Ireland, Lancashire, Yorkshire, Devonshire and other places, fires were lighted to commemorate the New Year, drive away witches and other malign forces, and many forms of divination were, practised appropriate to the beginning of the year"[2]. Frazer states that it seems to have been the time of year when "the souls of the departed were supposed to revisit their old homes in order to warm themselves by the fire." [3]

The Christian Church associated the ancient pastoral observances with its own feast of All Saints and solemnity of All Souls. Eventually it succeeded in altering the day of the "festival" but not its character. All Souls' Day is now the second instead of the first of November. And so in Christian times the "festival" became a church service

---

[1] "The Golden Bough – Balder the Beautiful" by James Frazer Vol. 1, (London: 1935) page 23.
[2] "Seasonal Feasts and Festivals" by E.O. James, (London 1961) page 310.
[3] "The Golden Bough" op. cit., page 225.

and its fiery aspect gradually disappeared.

But, in England, on November 5th 1605 Guy Fawkes and his fellow conspirators were discovered in their attempt to blow up Parliament. Guy Fawkes was a Roman Catholic and the Plot was said to be inspired by the Jesuits. The Government of James I encouraged the annual commemoration of its discovery, a special service for the "great deliverance" was included in the ritual of the English Book of Common Prayer and this was not excluded until 1859. The combination of religious fanaticism and the excuse to celebrate ensured the early success of the commemorative events. And after the Restoration a series of "Popish Plots" proved an excuse to revive the custom of burning effigies of the Pope and Guy Fawkes. It is interesting to note that although Fawkes was in fact hanged, his effigy is always burnt. Without the bonfires he would hardly have remained so famous a national villain.

In 18th Century London, the Green Ribbon Club held an annual bonfire pageant on November 17th, the anniversary of Queen Elizabeth I's accession. This club was violently anti-Catholic and part of the pageant was the custom of burning an effigy of the Pope at Smithfield with live cats in its belly to make realistic squalls.

Arthur Becket, the Sussex antiquary, writes about early pageantry in Lewes:-
"It is proved that the carnival had died down before the accession of James II, but on its revival during the days of that monarch it became an exceedingly popular event, and the burning of the Pope's effigy was a spectacle in which the common people took a peculiar delight. The figures of the Pope and Guy Fawkes were elaborately executed in wax, and the former was expensively clothed in a

handsome robe and tiara. Seated in a Papal chair this effigy was carried on a car in a procession of persons representing Cardinals and Jesuits. On the car stood a buffoon, disguised as a devil with horns and tail. After perambulating the town the 'pope' was presented to the flames amid the shouts of the populace. Even in those early days, no expense seems to have been spared in carrying out the carnival and the procession itself cost no less than £1,000." [4]

Becket does not give any references and his authority for this information is "a copy of an old pamphlet" given him by a Mr. William Banks of Southover, who is described as "The oldest Bonfire Boy in Lewes".

It is likely that some form of celebration did take place in Lewes, certainly it was an important town in a county which was famous for its extreme Protestantism. "That Puritanism was strong and widespread in Sussex may perhaps be inferred from the appointment of the famous and saintly Lancelot of Andrewes as Bishop of Chichester, or surely, of all the Churchmen of the time, he was the one most likely to win the Puritans into conformity with the Church's doctrine and practise." [5] Andrewes was appointed to Chichester in 1605 the year of the Gunpowder Plot.

The persecution of the Puritans under Charles I only strengthened their faith in Sussex, and Evelyn in his "Diary" complained that in the time of the Commonwealth most of the Sussex pulpits "were filled with Independents

---

[4] "The Spirit of the Downs" by Arthur Becket, (London 1909) page 212.
[5] "The Religious History of Lewes" by J.M. Connell, (Baxter, Lewes 1931) page 81.

and Phanaticles."

After the Restoration those ministers who did not adhere to the Act of Uniformity of 1602 were obliged to resign their livings. These men began to meet together with their followers despite the Conventicle Act of 1664, which imposed fines and other penalties on all who attended such meetings. In the Episcopal Returns for 1669 it is stated that there were three Conventicles in or about Lewes, a Presbyterian one at South Mailing, which numbered "at least five hundred", another in the Parish of All Saints described as "numerous" and one at Cliffe, numbering sixty. These Conventicles formed the nuclei of the nonconformist churches in Lewes.

And so there may be discerned a strong following for the extremist sleets of Protestantism in Lewes, by the beginning of the nineteenth century the following places of worship for dissenters had been erected in Lewes:-
    The Unitarian Meeting House (known as Westgate) founded in 1687
    The General Baptists' Meeting House, built in 1741
    The Old Chapel, Cliffe, built in 1775
    The Quakers' Meeting House, built in 1784
    The Particular Baptists' Meeting House, built in 1785
    The Wesleyan Chapel, built in 1788
    The Jireh Chapel, Cliffe, built in 1805
Such dissenters, by their very religious beliefs would have been unsympathetic to Catholic beliefs, and amongst their numbers may have been some who would keep alive any prevailing anti-Catholic sentiment in its extremist form. But, if so, there is no record of such demonstrations. I have not been able to find any reference to elaborate bonfire celebrations in Lewes before 1797.

CHAPTER II

> .....the paper fuse is quickly lit,
> A cat-like hiss, and spit of fire, a sly
> Falter, then the air is shocked with blast.
> 'Gunpowder Plot'. Vernon Scannell.

The Sussex Weekly Advertiser (published in Lewes) for November 6th 1797 contains the following report:-
"Yesterday being the anniversary of the Gunpowder Plot, the same was in the evening commemorated here by a large bonfire etc., being made on School Hill, as usual, but the conductors of it being threatened with a stout opposition they were somewhat more than ordinarily ceremonious in lighting it. The man appointed to that post, with a dark lantern in one hand, a match in the other, and a bundle of shavings hung across his shoulder, headed about forty others, walking in procession, with each a dried faggot on his shoulder and singing 'GOD SAVE THE KING', in which they were however, suffered to proceed without molestation, and we were glad to find that their triumph terminated without any mischievous consequence, beyond that of breaking a few panes of glass."

And so here we have the first description of a bonfire procession on November 5th in Lewes. It is obvious from the account that this was a normal occurrence, but there are no previous reports in this or any other local paper.

The following week's issue [6] contains a letter from one M. Adams: "Seeing in your Paper of the 6th inst. a short account of the proceedings etc. respecting the bonfire on School Hill on Sunday 5th we consider it an act of justice

---

[6] Sussex Weekly Advertiser, November 13th 1797.

to ourselves and the public to correct a mistake respecting the damages. In addition to eleven sash squares broken in Mr. Spilsbury's windows, by large stones thrown into the dining-room with rockets tied to them, it is to be added that several valuable articles are thereby much damaged and spoiled; and but for the vigilance of those in the house, who at the hazard of broken heads succeeded in extinguishing the fire, Mr. Spilsbury's house must have been in flames. Fortunately for us and our family, our house being very wet did not take fire, which nothing else could have prevented, as the bonfire was not the space of thirteen feet from it, with the wind from the South blowing the flames directly thereon'....'upon looking out of the window, a person (as if to intimidate) took a hat full of fire coals and strewed them close up to the house, then threw into the chamber a burning rocket, which narrowly missed my face...."

This element of rowdyism was to be an important point of dispute between celebrants and the law in future celebrations, and the following year the commemoration took place "regardless of the active exertions of our magistrates, Constables and the many Deputies appointed for their assistance, with the hope of preventing it." [7] And on the same day a blacksmith, concerned in letting off a bomb, had his thumb blown off "owing to his folly in holding it whilst it exploded." [8]

In the 1799 celebrations the rowdy excesses got out of hand and a boy and a servant girl were "dreadfully burnt" by having lighted squibs thrown at them. The authorities were taken to task by The Sussex Weekly Advertiser:- "Surely it is disgraceful to the Police that such acts of

---

[7] Sussex Weekly Advertiser, November 12th, 1798.
[8] Ibid.

wantonness and cruelty cannot be restrained". [9]

This behaviour obviously stirred the Police and prosecutions were brought to enforce the statute of 10th William III which imposed a penalty of £5 upon the vendor of squibs and of £20 on the persons using them.

In 1808 The Sussex Weekly Advertiser was happy to report that the Bonfire Boys, as they had come to be known "let off their crackers etc., with great cheerfulness, and without annoyance to anyone". [10] But the Advertiser was upset because many trees had been lopped and cut to supply fuel for the bonfires; "The juvenile perpetrators of these depredations we are inclined to think do not know that every such offence is FELONY and subjects the party committing it to the danger of TRANSPORTATION! [11]

For the next few years the citizens of Lewes were busy with the Napoleonic Wars and did not indulge in their annual celebrations. It has been suggested that the Bonfire Boys were able to continue their interest in pyromania by manning the beacon fires which were built to give warning of the expected invasion.

In 1821 William Plunkett introduced into the House of Commons a Catholic Emancipation Bill which passed the Commons but was thrown out by the Lords. In this year the celebrations in Lewes were resumed and The Sussex Weekly Advertiser observed that:-
"The excess of fireworks set off here on last Monday evening in commemoration of the Powder Plot, reminded us of former times; but without much consequent

---

[9] Sussex Weekly Advertiser, November 11th, 1799.
[10] Sussex Weekly Advertiser, November 7th, 1808.
[11] Ibid.

mischief, the only damage done being the accidental fracture of a few panes of glass in the coffee room windows, which had no shutters to defend them". [12]

It could be conjectured that the growing interest in the plight of Roman Catholics in this country, who still lived under legal disadvantages which were not repealed until 1829, may have incited extremists to re-star celebrations. In London there was an appearance of Orange Institution placards and bills which were profusely distributed in the City and West End calling Protestants to commemorate William Ill's birthday on 4th November. It is interesting to note in passing that some Protestants still commemorated the landing in England of William of Orange, which took place on the 5th. November 1688 and an annual service is still held at the Jireh Chapel in Lewes.

In 1823 the celebrations were held "with less vigour....than had been common on that occasion". [13] But in Southover "a rocket thrown from the street passed through a window of a chamber of Mr. Ellman's house, and set fire to the furniture of the bed whereon his children were sleeping; but happily it was observed and extinguished before it had time to do any mischief". [14] And this incident is recalled by one of the children, the Reverend Edward Boys Ellman in his book "Recollections of a Sussex Parson".

"Guy Fawkes Day is always a great day in Lewes, and the town on that night used to be given up to rioting. I recollect a rocket coining through the window and falling

---

[12] Sussex Weekly Advertiser, November 12th, 1821.
[13] Sussex Advertiser (name changed June 24th, 1822) November 10th, 1823.
[14] Ibid.

on the bed where I lay in the night nursery. Fortunately it was soon put out but many cases of fires through lighted fireworks being thrown through windows occurred and much damage was done. Some years later a Lewes butcher named Morris lost the sight of one of his eyes through a rocket being fired into a house." [15]

A letter from "A. Friend to Peace and Good Order" in The Sussex Advertiser refers to this "disagreeable and dangerous custom....It is thought by many, because the custom has been so long continued, that it has the sanction of the law." [16]

But although an element of religious intolerance was a feature of these celebrations the reason for the rowdy character of some of them is not difficult to discover. Lewes was the centre of an important agricultural area. And since 1815 a series of bad harvests and fluctuating prices for corn had led to bankcruptcy for many farmers and abject poverty for their labourers. The Times for 25th November 1830 quotes a petition presented on the 17th November from the agricultural labourers of Ringmer, near Lewes, to Lord Gage and other local farmers and landowners in which they ask:-
"....whether 7d. a day is sufficient for a working man, hale and hearty to keep up that strength necessary to the execution of that labour he has to do?....Have we no reason to complain that we have been obliged for so long a period to go to our daily toil with only potatoes in our satchels, and the only beverage to assuage our thirst is the cold spring; and on returning to our cottages to be welcomed by the meagre and half-famished offsprings of our bodies?....We therefore ask for married men 2s.3d. per

---

[15] Page 26 (1925 edition published by Cambridge, Hove).
[16] November 10th, 1823.

day to the 1st March and from that period to the 1st October 2s.6d. a day; for single men 1s.9d. a day to 1st March and 2s. from that time to 1st October." The men expressed the fear that they might end up in the poorhouse, the overseers of which are described as "men callous to the ties of nature, lost to every feeling of humanity, and deaf to the voice of reason."

This discontent was widespread throughout Southern England and although rural misery had been responsible ever since 1815 for sporadic out-breaks in years of exceptional distress, the agricultural uprisings of 1830 were on a far larger scale than any that had occurred before. "There was behind them no formulated common programme but almost everywhere the outbreaks followed much the same course. The labourers destroyed the threshing-machines and other new implements which reduced the demand for labour....Throughout the whole affair the labourer neither killed or wounded one single person. But their moderation did not save them when the Government, with the aid of the soldiers who were sent into the rural districts got the upper hand. Special Commissioners of judges were sent cut to try the offenders. Nine men were hanged, four hundred and fifty-seven transported and nearly as many more sent to prison for varying terms." [17]

It is not surprising that feelings ran high on Bonfire night in Lewes.

---

[17] "The Common People" by G.D.H. Cole and R. Postgate, (London 1962) page 240.

CHAPTER III

....the harvest sky,
Is flecked with threshed and glittering golden rain.
'Gunpowder Plot'. Vernon Scannell.

The celebrations continued as an outlet for high-spirits and dissatisfaction. In 1832 there was a "display of squibs and other fireworks, in the High Street, to the great annoyance of travellers, in addition to which lighted tar-barrels were rolled about the town, which the officers, very speedily, put a stop to." [18] But perhaps the citizens of Lewes were losing patience with this annual display of rowdyism because the Advertiser continues in caustic vein: "The march of intellect has not yet been able to prevent the celebration of this powder-plot tomfoolery."

In the next few years the events were marked occasionally by rioting but always by minor disorders. In 1841 Superintendent Flanigan and his Special Constables were attacked by armed Bonfire Boys. At the following assizes over twenty of the rioters were sent to prison for terms up to two months. This seems to have quietened the rowdier celebrants, for next year the event "continued with moderation and unaccompanied by any disposition to riot or breach of the peace" [19] and the crowds stood outside the residence of the High Constables and gave them "three times, three hearty cheers."

But this atmosphere of high-spirited enjoyment did not last long. Protestants had accepted the Catholic Emancipation Act of 1829, but in the forties they saw a gradual acceptance of Roman Catholic rites in some Church of

---

[18] Sussex Advertiser, November 12th, 1832.
[19] Sussex Advertiser, November 8th, 1842.

England services, the growing strength of the Oxford Movement, and the promise of the establishment of a Roman Catholic Hierarchy in England. This was too much for some Protestants, and Lewes was a centre for Protestants; for besides its seven Anglican churches it had Baptist, Wesleyan, Unitarian, Calvinistic Independent and Quaker Chapels. A spirit of anti-Catholicism was detected in the Lewes celebrations of 1843 by The Sussex Express which commented:-
"Since O'Connell and the Irish priesthood have denounced their fellow-subjects, the English, as Saxon tyrants, the desire for celebrating the fifth of November in this town has increased among many of its respectable inhabitants, under the impression that Popery still retains its ancient spirit of persecution and despotism and that it behoves all who value Protestant rights and privileges to show, in every possible manner their determination to resist its encroaches, whether directly through Papist or insidiously through the Puseyite." [20] This resurrected reason for holding the celebrations gave new force to the rowdyism of some of the celebrants.

On 5th November 1846 there was a particularly outrageous example of mob violence. Some hundreds of men and boys, mostly disguised, and carrying sticks and staves, marched through the town, and then organised a race through the streets with flaming tar-barrels dragged behind them. The mob then proceeded to the house of Mr. Blackman, a local magistrate and piled a number of tar-barrels in front of the building and set them alight. Mr. Blackman tried to remonstrate with the mob and to take one of them into custody, but on attempting to do this "another of the crowd dealt him a heavy blow over the eye with a bludgeon, and he fell to the ground apparently

---

[20] Sussex Express, November 11th, 1843.

lifeless. The magistrate was taken within doors in a condition of insensibility, his recovery being slow and attended with much suffering." [21] Suprisingly there is no record of charges being brought against the culprits but their behaviour incited "An Old Inhabitant" to publish a pamphlet entitled "Observations on the Doings in Lewes on the Evening of the 5th November 1846, with a Few Words to the Parties Interested." This pamphlet was an attack on the saturnalia and an appeal to the inhabitants to discontinue further demonstrations:-
"Another anniversary of the 5th November is past; it was accompanied by all the usual disgusting parade of disguises, bludgeons, and riots, the burning of tar barrels, thirty or upwards in number, fireballs, with rockets and the general description of fireworks; the whole trade of the High Street virtually at an end about six o'clock, and by seven, or soon after, the first tar-barrels made their appearance and continued till half-past eleven, and it was half-past twelve before the mob dispersed and the remains of the fire were put out."

"An Old Inhabitant" goes on to describe the Bonfire Boys as a "set of ruffians" and "ignorant ragamuffins" who brought annual disgrace to the respectable town of Lewes. He called on the Earl of Chichester and the other magistrates on the Lewes Bench "to give the whole matter their most serious consideration" reminding then that under the statute 46 George III "commonly called the Town Act....there is a clause in page sixteen inflicting a penalty not exceeding forty shillings, for assisting or abetting in making any bonfire, or letting off, firing, making selling etc., any crackers, squibs or other fireworks."

---

[21] Sussex County Magazine, November 1928, page 488.

The author states that no individual inhabitant of the town dare allow himself to be suspected of being unfavourable to the demonstrators, if so, he was a marked man liable to personal ill-use and insult, his house was liable to be beset and tar-barrels burnt before it. He points out that trade was affected by the carnival and that prospective inhabitants of Lewes may well be dissuaded from taking up residence "on seeing the accounts of the excesses committed here on the 5th November."

He concluded by hoping that all concerned and able to do so would follow "the dictates of their conscience" and do their duty in ridding the town of Lewes of "this abominable and disgraceful nuisance." If they did so he was convinced that on the 5th November 1847 "Lewes may be as free from annoyance as any other large and respectable town in the Kingdom."

But in the following year there occurred the most memorable clash between Bonfire Boys and the law. In anticipation of renewed trouble one hundred and seventy of the principal tradesmen and "other respectable citizens" were summoned to be sworn in as Special Constables, eighty metropolitan policemen were drafted into the town, and Lord Chichester and Sir Henry Shiffner, two members of the bench of magistrates, came into the town to stay overnight. The Sussex Advertiser whose proprietor, Peter Bacon, was opposed to the celebrations published a parody of the Bonfire Song, in its issue of the 2nd November 1847, as a warning to revellers, it concluded:-
Remember, my boys, remember,
No run is allowed at "the Jug";
And the private rooms, in December,
Are decidely cool, though snug!
Whoever finds winter quarters there
Will remember the 5th for the future, I'll swear.

On the "tottle of the whole", then,
"Twere best to avoid the din,
Let every one of the bold men
Keep fast his doors within;
Lest he find too late when regrets of no use
For the sake of a Fawkes he's been made a great goose

Of the one hundred and seventy citizens who were summoned to be sworn in as Special Constables, one hundred and eight applied to be excused on the grounds that "the means proposed by the magistrates, for preserving the peace of the town, were not the best, inasmuch as if the special constables were employed, private feelings and interest would effectually check any exertion towards the apprehension of offenders which was calculated to entail serious injury on those Special Constables who were the means of such apprehension. " [22] Their fears for their own safety were re-affirmed on the night of 4th November when they were jeered and insulted by a mob outside the Star Hotel, where they held a Meeting. During the evening fireworks were discharged about the town and seventy men and boys rushed down the High Street with a lighted tar-barrel, only to be ambushed by the police who had inserted a chain across the bottom of the street. A scuffle ensued and the ringleaders were taken into custody. This did not augur well for the following night.

Crowds swarmed into Lewes the following day in expectancy of an outbreak of rowdyism. But the presence of so many extra guardians of the law resulted in only sporadic outbursts until about eight o'clock in the evening. Then the Brighton mail-gig came dashing along the High Street, a cracker was thrown at the horse which bolted.

---

[22] Sussex Advertiser, November 9th, 1847.

The gig driver was thrown out and a passing pedestrian was run over. This led to an excited mob assembling round the injured men. It seemed to the magistrates that there would soon be a serious outbreak of rioting and so Lord Chichester addressed the crowd "exhorting them to retire peaceably to their homes and pointing out that although the magistrates were desirous of abstaining from all coercion, they were determined to clear the streets." [23] The crowd was given five minutes to disperse and as only a few did so the police were ordered to fall into rank. On the word of command "the whole force wheeled simultaneously right and left across the street, the crowd immediately flying in all directions, as if a troop of cavalary had been at their heels." [24]

This manoeuvre was very effective and although stones were thrown at the police only two arrests were made and these seemed to have deterred further trouble-makers. But the Bonfire Boys were not to be restrained so easily, and for the next few weeks they paraded nightly through the streets with tar-barrels and fireworks and "presented scenes utterly disgraceful to any civilised place." [25] No attempt was made by the authorities to prevent these disturbances. The offices of The Sussex Advertiser were attacked by a mob on the evening of the 23rd November and many windows were smashed. The rowdyism of the annual event seemed little connected with Guy Fawkes or religious fanaticism. The Bonfire Boys were obviously determined to show their disagreement with proposals of the police to employ force in the suppression of the demonstration. The authorities realised that they must use other means if they wished to preserve peace. The Sussex

---

[23] Ibid.
[24] Ibid.
[25] Sussex Advertiser, November 23rd, 1847.

Express suggested that compromise would be the best policy for all, and when in the following year a deputation of Bonfire Boys called on a magistrate to request that they leave the custody of the town in their hands on the 5th November the magistrates agreed.

John Ellman, a local magistrate offered the use of part of his Wallands Estate for a celebration. This would ensure that the public streets would not be the scene of riotous behaviour. A large crowd attended the bonfire and firework display, which was financed by Ellman and by public subscription. A band was in attendance and the proceedings were carried off without any incidence of bad behaviour. This was on November 6th but the previous evening had not been so quiet. The Sussex Advertiser in an editorial commented:-
"It is not only with the deepest disgust but with feelings of positive shame that we are under the necessity of stating that throughout the evening of Sunday last, the streets of this town were constantly disturbed by the discharge of fireworks. Disgraceful as has been the conduct of those who have on former occasions violated the peace of our streets by their lawless disturbances we confess we had not thought so lowly of then as to suppose them capable of such an outrage upon the common decencies of life, not to say upon the religious feelings of this country, as indicated in their revolting desecration of the Sabbath on Sunday night. Such an instance of unbridled licence and unmitigated ruffianism is beyond the realm of words." [26]

The more extremist Bonfire Boys were determined not to be deprived of their annual outburst. It must have seemed to them that the happenings at Wallands would see the end of the old rowdy displays in the High Street. And the

---

[26] Sussex Advertiser, November 7th, 1848.

whole spirit of the Lewes celebration seemed to vanish in the comparative mildness of the display at Wallands. Two years later their fears were allayed.

CHAPTER IV

"....the happy deliverance of King James I and the three Estates of England, from the most traitorous and bloody intended massacre by Gunpowder."
Book of Common Prayer (deleted 1859)

In 1850 Pope Pius IX issued a Bull re-establishing the Roman Catholic Hierarchy in England. This action followed by the publication of Cardinal Wiseman's first pastoral aroused fierce indignation throughout the country. More than 6,700 addresses to Queen Victoria called upon her and the Government to resist "the late aggression of the Pope upon our Protestantism." In his history of Roman Catholicism E.I. Watkins states: A. tornado of no-Popery hysteria swept the country. It was led by Lord John Russell....In an open letter he expressed his agreement with the Bishop of Durham's protest against the Pope's "insolent and insidious" action. He repeated these sentiments in a speech at Guildhall. Throughout the country grotesque effigies of the Pope and Cardinal Wiseman were burned by jeering mobs." [27]

This was the event for which the Bonfire Boys were waiting. Far from being driven off the streets they were welcomed by the Protestant citizens of Lewes as a way of demonstrating their indignation. Here was the original reason for bonfire-making all over again supposed Papal

---

[27] "Roman Catholicism in England from the Reformation to 1950" by E.I. Watkins, (London 1955).

infiltration into Protestant England, and the Bonfire Boys did not let the opportunity pass. The Sussex Advertiser complained:-
"From six o'clock till midnight there was an unceasing discharge of fireworks of "all sorts and sizes." In the course of the evening a troop of ruffianly fellows armed with bludgeons, dragged several tar-barrels down the high street of course, to the imminent danger of all whom they might meet in their course shouting and halloaing like madmen. A bonfire was lighted opposite the Town Hall and a large number of persons assembled to witness the conflagration and its accompaniments. Late at night the rabble danced around the fire uttering the most discordant yells; the scene reminding one far more of the orgies of infuriated savages than of the "amusements" of even a semi-civilised people....We understand that the police were expressly ordered to keep out of the way, and we cannot learn that they were seen on duty during the prevalence of the riotous proceedings described." [28]

No charges were brought against any revellers and the public acceptance of the celebrations seams to have been taken as a permanent permission to return to the old customs connected with this saturnalia; from 1850 the Lewes Bonfire Boys made the public streets the scene of their demonstrations.

The revived element of anti-Catholicism was a feature of the celebrations in the next few years. Effigies of the Pope and Cardinal Wiseman were paraded through the streets preceded by a brass band, and were consumed in huge fires in front of the White Hart Inn. The Sussex Express commented that "since Dr. Wiseman's insolent usurpation the celebration of this anniversary has partaken to a much

---

[28] Sussex Advertiser, November 12th, 1850.

greater extent than formerly of an anti-Romanist character; and the substitution of the Cardinal for the almost forgotten Guy Fawkes seems inevitable." [29]

By 1853 the Bonfire Boys had attempted to form themselves into a recognisable group. In this year sixty of them were dressed for the celebrations "with considerable uniformity in Guernsey"[30], that is a Guernsey shirt of blue and white horizontal stripes. In Southover a grand procession was organised "which, headed by a band, a variety of banners bearing inscriptions and the effigy of an old gentleman in black at the end, seated on a blazing tar-barrel, really presented a most imposing spectacle. All Southover was at the windows as it went by, the Guernseys walking three and four abreast, with the greatest order....Passing along the road to Lewes, its numbers gradually increased as it advanced, the procession went up St. Mary's Lane and than entered the High Street, where three cheers were called for and heartily given. Passing up the High Street, we noticed that almost every window was lined with fair spectators, and the inscriptions on the banners ("No Popery", "Hurrah for the Crescent", Down with Czar", "Three cheers for the Bench"), the dangling legs, of the Old Pope, and the occasional glowing of an unlucky squib, rather too near to be pleasant, seemed to afford the greatest amusement. Indeed there is no festival in which high and low – rich and poor – so heartily, so honestly and really join, as this Fifth of November anniversary." [31]

This organised procession is regarded as the first appearance of the Lewes Bonfire Society, now known as

---

[29] Sussex Advertiser, November 8th, 1851.
[30] Sussex Advertiser, November 12th, 1853.
[31] Ibid.

the Borough Bonfire Society. It was properly officered and, as can be seen from the account of its first appearance, it maintained an orderliness of behaviour amongst its members. From the first it included topical events and personalities in its tableaux and this year "there were exhibitions of the popular feeling with regard to the Eastern question." [32]

Effigies of the Czar joined those of the Pope (Pius the Ninth) and Guy Fawkes and there was a "large Russian bear, modelled with a degree of artistic skill that must have made our hairdressers indignant at its ultimate transfer to the flames." [33]

The events of 1853 were unmarred by any of the old riotous behaviour no arrests were made, and the orderly behaviour of the Bonfire Boys received the approval of The Sussex Express which hoped that "....they will always persevere in this course for it is only by this that can be preserved the commemoration of the deliverance of the King and Parliament of England, who were as our Prayer Book well hath it "by Popish treachery appointed as sheep to the slaughter in a most barbarous and savage manner beyond the examples of former ages." [34]

There is a report in the same issue of the Sussex Express of a demonstration in the Cliffe. A German band from Brighton headed the procession and No-Popery banners, lighted tar-barrels, grotesque masks and squibs were all in evidence. The Cliffe Bonfire Society dates its origin from this year and it still retains the strong "No Popery" element which was a keynote of all the early societies.

---

[32] Ibid.
[33] Ibid.
[34] Ibid.

In 1855 was issued the first programme of proceedings of the Lewes Bonfire Society:

> The order of procession, of the Lewes Bonfire Society, for the fifth of November 1855, All to meet at the Pelham Arms Inn, at six o'clock Precisely:-

1. To form a procession four abreast and start at half-past six, with the band and two tar barrels, to go down the town, St. Mary's Lane, through the Crescent, to the Swan Inn, Southover.
2. The procession to start from the Swan Inn, Southover at a quarter before seven with the band, banners, 25 torches two large tubs and four tar barrels, three to be taken from the Pelham Arms.
3. Two sugar hogsheads, six tar barrels and 25 torches to start from the Pelham Arms Inn at half-past seven, to proceed to the bridge, one to be thrown into the river as usual, the remainder to be brought back to the County Hall and put on the fire.
4. Four tar barrels at a quarter-past eight to proceed down town though Albion Street, up Market Street, back to County Hall.

THE GRAND PROCESSION
The Staff Bearer
Commander in Chief and Officers
Seven Lieutenants with Signal Lights and torches
GUY FAWKES   EMPEROR OF RUSSIA.
Bishop of Newtown in full canonicals
Emperor of Austria   King of Prussia
Banner "No Popery"
Band
Banner "Inkerman Anniversary"
Torch Bearers
Banner "Alma and Balaklava"
Torch Bearers

Banner "Sebastopol"
Torch Bearers
Banner "Bonfire Boys Arms"
Torch Bearers
Banner "Bonfire Boys coming out to night"
Six large Banners
Four large Sugar Hogsheads
Eight Tar Barrels
(Drawn by Harberd's party)
Banner "Success to the Bench"
Banner "God Save the Queen"
Mob.

6. Two sugar hogsheads and six tar barrels to be lighted at the Pelham and drawn to the Bridge, with band, banners and 25 torches.

7. Four tar barrels to be lighted at the Pelham Arms, to proceed down the Town, through Star Lane, down West Street up Market Street to the County Hall.

8. Three tar barrels to start from the Pelham Arms to the County Hall, with band; banners and the whole strength of the company singing and the band playing "GOD SAVE THE QUEEN."

The spirit of patriotism which had swept the country over the Crimean War was suitably reflected in the celebrations, and momentarily the crowds forgot that other potentate, the Pope, whilst they burnt Emperors of Russia and Austria and the King of Prussia. An added piquancy was given to the occasion because on the 5th November 1854 at the Battle of Inkerman "did a handful of Britains brave sons of freedom, defy the countless hordes of the Russian despot, and by their indomitable valour save not only the Queen and all her Parliament, but their country at large from the degradation of yielding to the serf-soldiers of the enemy." [35]

In such a spirit of xenophobia the "loyal Bonfire Boys of the Loyal Borough of Lewes" demonstrated before "many thousand spectators" and earned the approval of The Sussex Express once again. The editor of The Sussex Advertiser, Peter Bacon, had given up his fight against the proceedings after his effigy as a pig labelled "Peter the Papist" had been burnt in the demonstrations of 1852. He gives the celebrations scant notice from that year on.

A feature of the demonstrations introduced by the Cliffe Society in 1856 was the "Lord Bishop" who "officiated." He wore full clerical uniform and gave a "sermon" before the effigies ware burnt. The "sermon" usually consisted of a series of comments on topical events laced with a strong anti-Catholic tone. The wearing of sacred vestments upset many of the citizens who thought that the impersonation was "very questionable"[36] but this became accepted as part of the demonstrations. The obvious ritualistic aspect of the demonstrations was becoming more pronounced with the presence of such a priest".

In 1856 there is a mention of separate celebrations and bonfires in Commercial-square, and these probably saw the start of that Society.

By 1857 there were celebrations by the following societies, Lewes Town, which held the usual large parade in the town centre; Commercial Square, which joined the "grand procession" and then held its own bonfires; Waterloo Place, which had "tar-barrel runs" around its nearby streets; Cliffe, which had its separate celebration in

---

[35] Sussex Express, November 10th, 1855.
[36] Sussex Express, November 8th, 1856.

its own area.

The demonstrations of 1857 ware dominated by the news from India regarding the Fall of Delhi and effigies of sepoys and a "King of Delhi" were duly burnt to express the crowds feelings about yet another set of foreigners. But "No Popery" was still the cry, and a sidelight on the extent of anti-Catholic feeling in Lewes can be found in the account of an extraordinary scene, which took place on 18th November 1857.

The Rector of All Saints, Lewes, the Rev. John Scobell, had a daughter who had entered the Society of St. Margaret an Anglican order of nuns, better known as the Sisters of Mercy. This order had been founded by the Rev. J.M. Neale, a follower of Dr. Pusey, who had been suspended by the Bishop of Chichester for his "Romanist tendencies." Miss Scobell died, from scarlet fever, on 13th November at the Order's convent in East Grinstead. The circumstances of her death must have excited the imagination of the extremist Protestants of Lewes, for when her body was brought to Lewes, by the Rev. Neale and eight of the Orders sisters, they were greeted at the station by cries of "No Popery" from a large crowd.

After the body had been interred in the family vault the Rev. Neale requested that he should be allowed to enter. This request was not granted by the Rev. Scobell and this led the Rev. Neale to demand entry. A large crowd had accompanied the coffin to the vault (a recess in the wall of All Saints at the extreme north-east end of the churchyard) and on the Rev. Neale's request being rejected this crowd started to jeer and shout at him and the eight sisters. An "eye-witness" reported in The Sussex Express that "taunts" were made such as "Bring him another glass of brandy and wine", "Get a tar-barrel to warn

him"....wreaths were thrown up in the air, and cries of "No Popery", "Down with the Pope", and "Remember, remember the 5th of November" were heard on all sides." [37] The Rev. Neale was pushed and hustled out of the church yard, he was thrown to the ground and his gown torn from his back. Some of the sisters were taken pity on by the crowd, but others were lost in the mob, only to be re-united with the Rev. Neale in the public-house, the Kings Head, where they waited for nearly an hour whilst a siege was maintained by a mob of several hundreds. Eventually Neale escaped by climbing over two walls, nine feet high at the back of the public house and reached the Railway Station where he "borrowed a hat and coat." He was joined by the Sisters and they all left Lewes by the 7.40 train for East Grinstead. The Sussex Express summed up:-
"Thus ended an extraordinary and painful manifestation of the inherent hatred the laity have to any approximation to Popery." [38]

The mob element in this demonstration was a sad reflection on the orderly spirit which now dominated the bonfire celebrations. The proximity of the event to the 5th November had allowed the wilder elements to stage a further display of "No Popery".

In 1859 the Lewes Town Bonfire Society changed its name to the Borough Bonfire Boys Society and began to have regular meetings before the actual celebrations. The old Guernsey shirts were gradually being replaced by original "fancy-dress" costumes and these have continued to the present day. The Sussex Express described the costumes as fluctuating between the "general notion of a

---

[37] Sussex Express, November 21st, 1857.
[38] Ibid.

Greek warrior and Chickasaw Indian, a helmet, more or less fanciful being a very favourite appendage." [39] The revellers marched in procession carrying torches that gave off blue and red lights, which together with the light from the sugar hogsheads and the tar barrels gave and effect which was as "wild and grotesque as usual." The crowds of "2,500 at each bonfire" seamed undeterred by heavy rain and especial vigour was put into burning the effigy of that year's most hated foreign potentate, the Emperor of China "for what human heart can conceive anything more horrid and appalling than the atrocities that have been perpetrated on the brave defenders of our country's flag by the Chinese commanders and their men." [40] The reference to the war in China, in which the British Expeditionary Force had suffered heavy losses, continued the idea of comment on topical events, which gave the celebrations new life each year, and gave the Bonfire Boys an exercise in the use of their imagination away from the rather boring reiteration of anti-Catholic slogans.

The Commercial Square Bonfire Society made an appeal through its "officiating priest" ("the Lord Bishop of St. John's") for a "liberal subscription to the funds" from all those who had the same opinion as itself about preserving the celebrations as a "jovial gathering". So the tableaux, squibs, costume, etc., were financed by donations from the public; but the Cliffe Bonfire Society was unfortunate in 1858 when one of its members made off with the moneybox. He was commemorated the following year by being burnt in effigy along with the Pope and "old Neale". The Cliffe's celebration was made even more effective by the costumes of its members which included suits of armour

---

[39] Sussex Express, November 8th, 1859.
[40] Ibid.

and which "far exceeded that of any previous year." [41]

CHAPTER V

...the frenzied whizz of Catherine-wheel
Puts forth its fiery petals.
"Gunpowder Plot". Vernon Scannell

By the 1860's a lot of the old boisterous spirit of the celebrations had evaporated. This spirit was associated with the anti-Catholicism of earlier days, but when in 1859 the Service of Thanksgiving, prepared in 1605, was deleted from the Book of Common Prayer, this could be taken as a sign of more tolerant times. The violent outbursts against the re-establishment of the Roman Catholic Hierarchy, in England had failed in their purpose, and it was natural that with the passing of the years much of the excitement that attended earlier demonstrations should have died down. Now that the various societies had become established an air of respectable orderliness attended the celebrations, "We ought here to add that the celebration was conducted with every decorum, and so far from any attempt being made to destroy property or commit a breach of the peace, there appeared every disposition on the part of the Bonfire Boys to preserve both." [42]

The bonfire societies prepared effigies of Louis Napoleon, "King Bomba" (the King of Naples) and Victor Emmanuel to be consigned to the flames along with the Pope. Their banners contained political slogans on behalf of the oppressed in foreign lands ("Success to Garibaldi" and "No Slavery" in America) but these opinions could not be

---
[41] Ibid.
[42] Sussex Express, November 10th, 1860.

expressed with such fervour as were those against that supposed oppressor of religious liberty in England. It is difficult to imagine people who were politically powerless in England ("Britains never will be slaves" said one banner in 1862) demonstrating on behalf of their fellows in far distant lands. But there is no record of any demonstrations demanding their own political liberty, and yet most of the demonstrators were of the "mob"; and the "officers" of the societies were small tradesmen, who were not enfranchised until 1867.

A study of the programmes issued at this period by the societies shows that the order of processions was unchanged from year to year. In fact it became the habit to reprint the previous years programme with no changes. And the officials of the various societies remained in their office for many years, usually until they died and they were succeeded by their sons. So a rather unimaginative spirit may be discerned in the proceeding which acquired a sameness over the years.

Despite the absence of the old religious fervour the celebrations continued; but without any unusual incidents. In 1867 a Roman Catholic chapel was established in Lewes and a couple of years later the Bonfire Boys burnt an effigy of Pope Pius IX outside it. But the old spirit of animosity seemed to have vanished. The year 1874 saw a change in the annual celebration when a minor out-break of typhoid fever caused the Societies to delay the event until the 31st December. The spectacle of the richly clad revellers parading through the streets in a snow-storm was a memorable occasion which probably saw the final establishment of the event as a carnival rather than a religious demonstration.

By the end of the century (1892) the Southover Society

was formed to be followed in (1893) by the St. Anne's Society. These joined in the general celebrations which were lead by the Borough Bonfire Society and then like the other societies returned to their own part of the town for separate bonfires.

In 1894 the strength and organisation of the various societies may be discerned by looking at the programmes for that year. The grand procession of the Borough Bonfire Society was as follows:

Pioneers   Chief Pioneers   Pioneers
Pioneers   Chief of Pioneers   Pioneers
Colours "Union Jack"
Staff Officers   Staff Officers
Staff Marshall Staff Bearer Staff Marshall
The Commanders-in Chief
Groom in waiting   Staff Bugler   Groom in waiting
Chief of Staff
Field Marshalls   Field Marshalls
Staff Surgeon   Aide-de-camp   Staff Surgeon
Ambulance Staff
Inspectors General   Inspectors General
THE LORD BISHOP OF LEWES
With attendant body-guard of Veteran Boys
The Ancient Key of the Borough of Lewes
Staff Officers   Staff Officers
Grand new banner designed by our own Special artist
Captain of the Band
The Society's celebrated Military Band in Costume
Banner
"May we never engage in a bad cause or flinch from a good one"
Captain of Tableau
MAGNIFICENT TABLEAU

Representing the Ancient Temple of Titi-put-tu, surmounted by the Sacred Dragon of China and containing the Fire Idol "Ting Ling" who having been fed on Lewes Rousers eventually becomes too fiery and disappears from this planet in flame and smoke, being assisted on his journey by the aforesaid dragon
   Yeoman of the Tableau Yeoman of the Tableau
Banner
EFFIGIES OF GUY FAWKES & THE POPE
Ancient banner "No Popery"
Captain of Ranks Captain of Ranks
Lieutenants of Ranks
Borough Boys Borough Boys
"Parish Councillors" in appropriate costume
Attended by numerous members of the Society with Fireworks, coloured Fire and Torches.
Banner
The Commercial Square Bonfire Society with Band
Banners, torches, Hogsheads and Tar barrels

Members of other Bonfire Societies
Captain of Tubs
Lieutenant of Tubs   Lieutenant of Tubs
With Blazing Hogsheads and Tar Barrels

This imposing array of costumes and brilliant lights over 1,000 people and was one mile long. At the end of the procession through the streets the "Lord Bishop of Lewes" gave an address which covered a wide range of topics, including a condemnation of the doctrine of Papal Infallibility, an expression of sorrow at the death of Alexander III of Russia, and a thorough condemnation of the "stupidity of magistrates at Glasgow and Birmingham in ordering the destruction of beautiful works of art because they included nude figures." [43] So this annual diatribe allowed the "Bishop" to express his opinions on unrelated subjects without opposition; and to conclude by calling for hearty cheers for the Queen, the Prince, the Princess of Wales, the Mayor and the Mayor-elect.

But some people in Lewes did not approve of the way in which the religious aspect of the celebrations was being forgotten or only mentioned in passing. In the same year the minister at Southover Church, the Rev. W.E. Richardson instituted an annual "Thanksgiving for deliverance from the Popish Plot" service for the Sunday nearest to "Guy Fawkes Day". This service was discontinued by his successor but was restarted at the Jireh Chapel in 1912 and is still held there. The discourse consisted of expressions of anti-Catholic sentiment, but may be presumed to have been heard only be the converted and certainly had no major effect on the celebrations, although many leading Bonfire Boys attended the service in an "official" capacity.

In 1901 there was erected at Southover a memorial to the Protestant martyrs and this was the occasion in November of that year for a last all out effort to enfuse a spirit of anti-Catholicism into the celebrations. But the extremists were not successful and the spirit of carnival predominated despite the Rev. Richardson of Southover and the Southdown Loyal Orange Lodge.

A fire in the High Street in September 1904 resulted in the police issuing a request to the societies, now formed into the Amalgamated Bonfire Societies of Lewes, to restrict the use of fireworks amongst their members. The "warning" which they issued marked a definite change in

---

[43] Sussex Advertiser, November 9th, 1894.

the nature of the celebrations:-

"We the undersigned, being duly authorised by our respective Societies wish it to be generally known by all concerned, that we have resolved to discountenance the letting off of all kinds of explosive fireworks, including large Roman Candles, on the night of Saturday the 5th November. We therefore request that all well-wishers of the cause will loyally co-operate in assisting the members of the Societies in this direction. We earnestly hope that our friends will recognise the spirit in which this notice is issued and do their utmost to make the celebration this year the beat on record".

The celebrations of that year were but a shadow (or perhaps ember) of those of the previous years. With the Bonfire Boys themselves issuing such a warning the old spirit must have collapsed. Times had indeed changed from those days when the Bonfire Boys had fought policemen, and openly defied the authorities to keep them off the streets. The bonfires were very small and the processions were mere caricatures of those of previous years. There was no thunder in the "Bishop's" address and banners merely said "We are Protestants" instead of the dogmatic "No Popery". The Sussex Express gave vent to the feeling at the time "Bonfire is Dead, Long live the memory of the glorious "Fifths" that have been." [44]

1905 was the three-hundredth anniversary of the Gunpowder Plot. But there was no special effort made to give an extra sparkle to the celebrations. The Societies adhered to their declaration to restrict the use of fireworks, and the popular belief was that this would be the last of the commemorations on the "old historic lines". The programme for the Borough Bonfire Society gives a time-

---

[44] Sussex Express, November 11th, 1905.

table for the evening showing that the Societies now cooperated so that the public could see each of the main bonfires with the effigies being destroyed:

Time p.m.	Society	Procession Etc.
6.00	Borough	First torchlight Procession starts
6.45	Borough	"St. Anne's Grand" starts
7.30	Borough	School Hill Procession starts
7.45	Commercial	"Wallands Grand" starts
7.45	Southover	"Grand" starts.
8.00	Southover	Effigies destroyed
8.15	Cliffe	"Grand" starts
8.30	Cliffe	Effigies destroyed
9.15	Borough	"Town Grand" starts
9.45	Borough	Effigies destroyed
10.00	Commercial	"Grand" starts
10.40	Commercial	Effigies destroyed
11.15	Borough	Final

"A fire will be kept up opposite the County Hall during the whole of the evening." And there is an advertisement in the programme for "Eye Protectors from 2½d per pair." But the event passed off quietly and the only effigies were those of those hardy perennials Pope Paul V and Guy Fawkes.

In 1906 even the smaller fires were banned in the streets and this was a severe blow to the Societies and especially to the morale of their members. With the bonfires went the whole spirit of "Bonfiredom". The St. Anne's Society and the Southover Society ceased to function, and the famous Borough Society was forced to amalgamate with the Commercial Square Society.

The Bonfire Boys were determined to fight "the dying of the light" verbally if not with fisticuffs. Addressing the crowd at the combined Commercial Square and Borough Society's fire which was pitched in a field, just beyond Lewes Prison the "Bishop" said:-

"I need hardly remind you that previous to last year's celebrations the county police authorities issued orders which, had they been enforced would have prevented the proceedings being carried out in the usual way, but as the preparations were far advanced the matter was allowed to remain in abeyance. Perhaps it is not so well known, however, that such orders were the outcome of a petition signed, it is believed, by not more than 100 persons, of whom some, it is also believed, were not residents of Lewes. Such a petition could not claim to represent the feeling of the town and while many of the signatories were no doubt genuinely apprehensive of the injury to person and property (the risk of which was perhaps much magnified) yet the notoriously extreme views of those who engineered the petition would warrant us looking much deeper for the true motives underlying this opposition."

The "Bishop" believed that various Roman Catholics amongst the county police officials were responsible for the sterner view now taken by the authorities of fires in the streets. Perhaps they had detected a resurgence of anti-Catholicism instigated by the Orange Lodge, which had presented new "No Popery" banners to the societies.

Whatever the reason 130 policemen wore on duty in the town that night and 14 people were arrested for discharging fireworks. Amongst those arrested were 4 of the leading Bonfire Boys of that time. William Gearing, Thomas Gearing, Eli Dawe and Harold Weston, were duly summonsed to appear before the magistrates on a charge of having "unlawfully assembled to disturb the public peace and to cause alarm and then did make a great disturbance to the terror and alarm of His Majesty's subjects there being and against the Peace of our Sovereign Lord the King, his Grown and Dignity." They had in fact thrown torches onto the roadway and those had been regarded as bonfires by the police. The police maintained that the signal for the torches to be thrown down had been a roll on a drum. But the drummer maintained that this had been a signal to the band to strike up with the National Anthem, so the case was dismissed.

The celebrations never recovered their old splendour after this concerted action by the police. Like so many other rural pleasures of previous ages it was to decline into the insipidity of a Twentieth century entertainment, lacking enthusiasm which characterised the earlier carnivals. But there was always the hard core of enthusiastic members in the societies who carried on the tradition of costume-making and preparing the torches.

Each society had members who wore experts in tableau constructing. Preparations for the carnival would begin about two months before the 5th November, and each society would make about five hundred torches of tarred rope wound into sticks about 2 feet long and fastened with wire.

The womenfolk would make the costumes and these were carefully preserved and used year after year. As most of the revellers were from the poorer homes these costumes must have been highly prized. The only contemporary printed account of a bonfire society's meeting before 5th November is given by Arthur Becket in his book "The Spirit of the Downs":-[45]

"The headquarters of the Bonfire Societies are at local hotels; and at the first meeting of members for the year the

---

[45] "The Spirit of the Down" op. cit. page 222.

secretary cries "The books are open", and those present throw coins on to the table, as much as £20 sometimes thus being collected in an evening. The officials are elected; and in Lewes it is considered great honour to hold office in one or other of the societies. Collectors are then appointed to visit the inhabitants whose response is free and unstinted." The money collected beforehand and that collected during the procession defrayed the expense of purchasing fireworks and making torches etc. All the money collected was spent on the celebrations; the present day habit of collecting for charity did not emerge until after the First World War.

In 1909, the Borough Society and the Commercial Square Society severed their amalgamation and celebrated with their own bonfires. And The Sussex Daily News was able to report that:-
"These celebrations have now settled down to an orderly torchlight parade of the streets in fancy dress, but although the boisterous behaviour of the past is no longer possible in the streets, it must not be imagined that these are ordinary torchlight processions. They are unsurpassed as a bustling nocturnal spectacle. Their brilliance and the excellence of their organisation are alike wonderful, and it is not surprising that hundreds still come into town from neighbouring places to witness the celebrations." [46]

The Sussex Daily News also reported that the smaller celebrations in other Sussex towns and villages "were not particularly numerous." But it is interesting to note that the collections made at these celebrations were made on behalf of various charities, whilst those in Lewes still went to finance the tableaux and fireworks of the Societies.

---

[46] The Sussex Daily News, November 6th, 1909.

In 1913 the last celebrations before the First World War seemed to be part of that "Age of Golden Sunlight" that was coming to an end. The carefree concern of the revellers makes a strong contrast with what would be their attitudes a year later. The Sussex Daily News reported: "The evening was beautifully fine, and the whole proceedings were not marred by anything of an unfortunate character. The effects produced by the various processions ware exceedingly pretty, though at times quite grotesque. The Borough Society had arranged seven processions in all, the "grand procession", was a magnificent one, and the variety of fancy costume unique. The tableau was entitled "Caught in the act", and represented a lady, evidently of the suffragette persuasion, standing at the door of a church and carrying a mysterious-looking article labelled "bomb. Two constables, human ones, had evidently caught her in the act. The Church and the lady "fired" splendidly. The customary effigies of Guy Fawkes and the Pope also proved to be well set. The procession itself was led by pioneers and the country's defenders and guardians of its souls were all strongly represented." [47]

The Cliffe Society confined their effigy to the "The Popish Pedlar", in whose hand there was a rosary, showing that one tradition had not died. Whilst the Commercial Square Society had effigies in contemporary costumes. "Some were intensely amusing skits on the current fashions, feminine particularly, the aigrette was to the front, and the "nut" came in for his full share of representation." [48] At the end of the evenings celebrations the band of the Borough Society played "Auld Lang Syne" as the last embers of the bonfires were doused by the local fire

---

[47] Sussex Daily News, November 6th, 1913.
[48] Ibid.

brigade. It was to be six years until they "remembered" again.

CHAPTER VI

> The Cannon bangs and in my nostrils drifts
> A bitter scent that brings the lurking past
> Lurching to my side.
> "Gunpowder Plot". Vernon Scannell

After the War the citizens of Lewes would have been too busy "picking up the threads" to prepare for an event which was a mere spark compared with what some of them experienced in battle. The Cliffe Society was the only one to organise a procession and this was surprisingly shorn of its previous element of religious bigotry. There was no effigy of the Pope (Catholics had, of course, fought alongside Protestants against a common foe) and the "Lord Bishop" had become the "Lord High Chancellor". The main tableau depicted "Kaiser Bill's Ride to London" which was the exclusive design of Bonfire Boys of the Cliffe who had returned from active service. There were three separate processions, but heavy rain fell and dampened the enthusiasm of the participants.

By 1924 the Borough Society and Commercial Square Society reformed and the Southover Society, long defunct, also joined in the celebrations. An offshoot of the Cliffe, the Cliffe Juvenile Society took part in the 1924 celebrations. The old habit of commenting upon contemporary political events was begun again in the tableaux. A patriotic and anti-German note was struck by the Commercial Square Society with a tableau entitled "Wanted, a closed gate", the idea being that there should be a closed gate against the importation of German goods into this country. The Borough Society also commented on the subject with its tableau entitled "The Burning Question: All alone". In 1926 the St. Anne's Society was restarted after twenty years and all the societies joined a council called the Lewes District Council of Bonfire Societies. The main result of the central council was that in future the collections made on the evening of 5th November, whilst the processions made their way through the streets, was to be given to charity after deduction of expenses. This decision gave the last touch of respectability to the proceedings and effectively prevented any criticism of its continuance in public streets.

The absence of any extravagant display of anti-Catholicism did not last for long. The Defence of the Realm Act had dissuaded even extremist revellers from indulging in giving public insult to their fellow citizens. But even after its repeal the new Bonfire Council agreed that anti-Catholic demonstrations were no longer desirable, nor suitable in post-war Britain. But in 1930 the Cliffe Society, always the leading anti-Catholic Society in the past, burned an effigy of "a pope" outside the Catholic Church in Lewes during the celebrations. This lead to the Town Council asking all Societies to discontinue the practice of burring the Pope's effigy. In fact no society other than the Cliffe, had burnt such an effigy sine 1921 and it was the Cliffe, now that refused to agree to the Council's request. It resigned from the Bonfire Council, and it still burns the Pope's effigy accompanied by the public recitation of the Bonfire Prayer. [49] The Borough Society stated in its programme for 1932 that "The religious significance of our celebration has faded into the past, where it rightly belongs."

The societies showed themselves aware of what was

---

[49] Printed here in the Appendix.

happening outside Lewes when the Borough Society had as its tableau for 1936, Hitler disguised as the Wolf in Grandma's clothing and Britain disguised as Red Riding Hood. And in 1937 it had effigies of Hitler and Mussolini, which were consumed in the flames along with Guy Fawkes.

The last pro-war celebrations in 1938 saw the arrest of forty people for throwing fireworks, the burning-out of a car parked by a spectator and a great many casualties from burns. The tableaux again referred to the menaces to peace on the Continent, and the Cliffe Society had a gigantic volcano in tableau entitled "Eruption in Europe" which illustrated the spasmodic European troubles. But the "Bishop" of the St. Anne's Society made reference in his speech to the apathy of members in preparing for the celebrations, he feared that soon there would be an end to this traditional display. It had become the custom to give prizes for the best fancy dresses in each of the societies' processions and this was one way of keeping enthusiasm for the event. A prophetic tableau by the Southover Society was entitled "Will it happen?", it depicted "a village somewhere in England" being bombed by enemy planes.

When the real enemy planes threatened in the following year the celebrations were cancelled. Instead the societies observed "the Fifth" each year during the Second World War by placing a wreath on the Lewes War Memorial.

The first "Guy Fawkes Day" after the end of the hostilities was an obvious excuse to enter into the post-war spirit of carefree gaiety. Ironically there had been two Victory parades through Lewes during the summer of 1945 so that by the time November 5th came there was a scarcity of fireworks. But the societies put on a very creditable display and the event was made the lead story in the local newspaper for the first time in its existence. Four societies took part: The Borough, Commercial Square, Cliffe, South Street Juveniles. This latter Society was for children and the emphasis was on fancy dress, prizes being given for the best. The evening's proceedings opened with each society sending a representative to lay a wreath at the War Memorial. About 800 men, women and children then paraded through the streets in four separate processions. There was no joining in each society's procession by members of other societies as there had been in previous years, and the "archbishop" of the Cliffe Society annoyed some citizens by condemning the attitude of the Vatican during the war in his speech. Whilst the "Bishop" of the Borough Society challenged the Cliffe Society to prove that they were the oldest bonfire society in Lewes. This spirit of rancour amongst the societies was noted by The Sussex Express which referred to the "impressive display" but added that "it might have been more impressive still with co-operation among the Bonfire societies." [50]

In the following year the old mob spirit returned to the celebrations. The same four societies took part and the Commercial Square society had an enormous tableau "depicting the execution of Goering as it was planned". [51] A life-size effigy of Goering was shown hanging from a gallows. It was filled with forty pounds of gunpowder and when it was ignited the "huge explosion....sent the front row watchers surging back into the crowd for safety." [52] The Sussex Express commented that the "old days of bonfire" were returning to Lewes, and added that thousands of visitors had come to see the celebrations.

---

[50] Sussex Express, November 9th, 1945.
[51] Sussex Express, November 8th, 1946.
[52] Ibid.

Over 2,000 people took part in the four processions, and the societies reported that membership was increasing. But already there were suggestions that the societies should amalgamate to produce a "Grand Procession", as the cost of procuring fireworks and constructing tableaux was becoming prohibitive because of the small society funds.

It was still the practise of all societies to deduct expenses from the street collections and then to give the remainder to local charities. Money gifts from local traders were encouraged because the societies maintained that the celebrations drew publicity and, therefore, visitors and trade to Lewes.

In 1949 the celebrations were televised by the B.B.C. and this resulted in a more enthusiastic spirit among society members. The "Archbishop" of Commercial Square said in his speech that amalgamation of the Lewes Bonfire Societies would be a bad thing as it would destroy the competitive element, but he hoped that there would be co-operation in future years. The Cliffe Society instigated a juvenile Society in 1949, and continued their anti-Catholic tradition with a bitter attack on "an alien Church" whilst they burned effigies of Guy Fawkes and Pope Paul V "the one as being the tool of the Papal Conspirators against out national freedom, and the other as representing the system behind the diabolical plot", according to their "Archbishop" in his speech.

The Borough Society noted in its programme for 1949 that over £150 had been given to local charities from the joint collections since the war. It was still the custom for all societies to start the evening's proceedings by placing wreaths on the War Memorial. The celebration had now taken on an air of permanence and respectability and there is no record of any one objecting to its continuance. But the Cliffe Society was condemned in The Sussex Express for its anti-Catholicism in a world where that Church was seen as a leading bulwark against "the Red menace." [53]

Talks between the societies during 1950 lead them to stage a United Giant Procession in that year. The societies concerned were the Borough, Commercial Square, South Street and the newly re-formed Southover. The Cliffe held aloof, and stated in its programme that it intended that its celebration should have a meaning and not be a more carnival: "We should also mention that in carrying out our celebrations in the way we do, we consider we are giving very practical expression to the third paragraph of Article 37 of the Church of England (as contained in the Book of Common Prayer) which roads as follows:-"The Bishop of Rome hath no jurisdiction in this Realm of England."

The previous year's publicity by television resulted in over 12,000 visitors to Lewes on November 5th 1950. 49 people were arrested and buses were reported as being one hour behind schedule because of traffic jams. The Grand Procession was accompanied by seven bands and stretched for over one mile in length. Each of the "bishops" referred to rumours that the societies were "finished" and all promised that they were not and, in fact, membership was going "from strength to strength". But it may be seen in their programmes that each year saw the same parale of similar costumes and bands with the only variation being the theme of the tableaux: Goering in 1946, Communism in 1950. One is reminded of that dictum of Thomas Hardy when, in his account of the mummers at Christmas on Egdon Heath in "The Return of the Native", he remarks

---

[53] Sussex Express, November 11th, 1949.

that the genuine survival of a tradition can always be distinguished from the modern revival because in the former the performers will seem to be carrying out their annual task out of a sense of dreary obligation, whereas in the latter they will appear enthusiastic. It could be conjectured that the modern Bonfire Boys come under the former category.

Since 1950 the celebrations have occurred with an annual inevitability that has been accompanied by a gradual lessening of enthusiasm amongst public and the reveller. The growing popularity of television in this period has been blamed by the societies for the diminishing crowds on November 5th. A number of "Guy Fawkes Nights" have been completely, "washed out" by rain, and in 1960 the celebrations were cancelled when the town was flooded. In 1959 the Southover Society suspended operations as a separate society, although its place was taken in 1964 by the Waterloo Society, which had been defunct for nearly 60 years. But now the societies operated on a much smaller scale than in previous years. There wore no longer elaborate tableaux nor "speeches" about current affairs at the bonfire sites. 1952 saw the last of the big tableaux and these were confined to expressing the societies' loyalty to the new Queen.

In 1965 the grand united procession was dropped from the display, and the societies held their own processions in their own areas. The Evening Argus commented:-"The whole character of the celebrations in Lewes has changed. Not so long ago it was very much a family affair with parents taking their children and lining the streets to watch the many colourful processions. Now it is the teenagers who provide most of the spectators and they are more concerned with following a procession than being a static spectator."[54]

The newspaper reports of the celebrations at this time are given headlines such as "Quieter than usual" or "The all quiet bonfire night", and the space devoted to them is much less than in previous years.

The purpose of today's celebration is to collect money for charity by creating a spectacle which attracts visitors to the town by the thousands, and brings childlike delight to all.

APPENDIX

The Bonfire Prayer was a traditional rhyme in Sussex and is still recited at the Cliffe Bonfire Society celebrations. It is as follows:

> Please to remember,
> The Fifth of November,
> Gunpowder Treason and Plot,
> I see no reason
> Why Gunpowder Treason
> Should ever be forgot.
> Guy Fawkes, Guy,
> Twas his intent
> To blow up the King and his Parliament;
> Three score barrels laid below
> To prove old England's overthrow;
> By God's providence he was catch'd
> With a dark lantern and lighted match
> Holloa, boys, holloa boys make the bells ring,
> Holloa boys, holloa boys, God save the King.

---

[54] The Evening Argus, November 6th, 1965.

> A furden loaf to feed old Pope,
> A pen'worth o'cheese to choke him,
> A pint o'beer rense it down
> An' a faggot o'wood to burn him.
> Burn him in a tub o'tar
> Burn him like a blazing star,
> Burn his body from his head
> Then we'll say old Pope is dead!
> Hip, Hip, hoo-r-r-ray.

There is no full history of the celebrations in Lewes, but I must acknowledge my indebtedness to the privately published pamphlet "Bonfire" written by the late Bert Munt. I am very grateful to the staff of the Reference Department of Brighton Public Library for their expert and courteous assistance. I shall be glad to learn of further sources of information (and about my errors) from any readers who care to write to me c/o 4, Spences Lane, Lewes, Sussex.

******

Note from the editor of this current volume: Simon O'Halloran published this pamphlet in 1967 and since then there have been a few books published regarding the history of the celebrations in Lewes, see sources and further reading at end of this publication.

******

Lewes Bonfires 1908, 1909 & 1910
by Annette Philly Verrell

Historian Vol. 7 No 6, September 1987

Remember Remember the fifth of November.

I should like to remember the experiences of my first Bonfire Night. I had heard so much about it and Lewes is really the only place throughout Great Britain where the Gunpowder Plot and its meaning is told and illustrated year by year not only by burning torches and coloured fires being carried through the streets and by the burning of an enormous effigy of Guy Fawkes and Pope Paul, but there is always a Bonfire Service held the Sunday before in the Jireh Chapel, which is packed with loyal worshippers of the Catholic faith.

It is put very clearly to us all, the necessity of keeping Roman Catholics from getting a firm hold of our country and we are told that the Bonfire has been kept up year by year to commemorate the landing of William of Orange by a truly patriotic people. An enthusasm which is handed down from father to son and worked at with a zeal worthy of the cause. The effigies are really wonderful when one remembers they are chiefly composed of fire-works and coloured lights and are made by members of the Bonfire Society who labour far into the hours of the night after their actual day's work is done. I've been told it is very hard work indeed and is begun some months before the glorious "Fifth" comes.

Both years I have seen it the weather has been exceptionally fine and the first year all went well but last year, 1909, a man named Tom Gearing was seriously burnt and it ended in death two days later. He was a torch-bearer and after supplying the procession with torches at headquarters (the Elephant and Castle, for we have followed the Commercial Square Society) he was following in the rear with a bundle of torches in his arms and had on a striped woollen jersey which, of course, was saturated with paraffin and it is said that a man with a lighted torch collided with him and in a second the man was enveloped in flames. He was nearly mad with fright and pain but with all speed was driven off to the Victoria Hospital, where two days later he died, more from the severe shock than the actual burns. Day by day the Bonfire Boys made enquiries and a substantial relief fund was started by them for the widow and six children the youngest then only three days old. It met with a ready response and is now bringing the widow in fifteen shillings a week until her youngest child is fourteen besides living rent free. So they have done what they could.

I started with the idea of describing the pleasant time Nelly and I had together that night but find I have wandered from my purpose in trying to give an impression of what the Bonfire was really intended to remind us of. Also the poor man's story which I have told in a few words, because everyone was impressed by it and also his is the first life lost in Bonfire Celebration although it is carried out very much quieter now than it has ever been. Now they light the Bonfire and burn the effigies in an open field, whereas in years gone by it was lit in front of the Town Hall and at the principal street corners. The first procession passed here about six, there were men in every uniform of the army they could get, there were merry sailors, safer perhaps on land than sea. There were gorgeous princes of every tribe one could think of, resplendent in flying head-dress and a plentiful supply of jewels, each one carrying a lighted torch. Girls dressed in fancy costume to represent all nations and some of the dresses worn by both men and girls were well worth seeing and as anyone could see had been well thought out. Nelly and I were told to get supper in, which was hot, at seven o'clock and when they had finished and we had cleared away and washed up, and had prepared another supper for when the family and friends returned and had tidied all the bedrooms, we would then be at liberty to go out and enjoy the sights and they hoped we should get off early! We went just before nine wondering how much we had missed while we quickly made our way towards the Cliffe where we joined the procession, when, to our great delight we learnt that the lighted tar-barrel had not yet been thrown over the bridge. So we saw that, then during the interval while the Bonfire Boys were taking refreshments, we walked up St Ann's where we met two young men who had come in from Newhaven. They were pleasant company and good protectors, having on stronger boots than we had, to trample out the fragments of fire before it set light to our skirts.

The fire that year was along Offham Road in a large field and the crowds standing all along the banks watching the sight showed the interest taken by all, in Fifth Celebration. We got through nearer the fire to hear the Bonfire prayers being read and to see the flames consume the mighty effigy of Guy Fawkes first, afterwards that of Pope Paul. Then the splendid tableau. After this the Procession formed again and Nelly and I with our 'young gallants' followed. These fellows purposely lost their train, because if they had caught it, they would have missed the Bonfire as their train went at 11:10. So we made our way back along Offham Road behind a very merry party of young men, all dressed in farmers' smocks and singing lustily 'Sussex by the Sea' it was rather good too. My escort and Nelly's both came home with us although they had got to walk back to Newhaven that night, or rather, morning. We enquired of them their names and gave them ours and we both received letters telling us of the very pleasant evening they had spent and the moonlight walk they had home, no doubt, like us, talking over the events of the evening. I remember they signed themselves 'Your Bonfire Chum'.

Last year we did not find the Fifth quite so exciting although we both got out a little earlier but we met Nelly's Aunt who had never seen it before and she came with us. I fancy she was a trifle nervous of the lavish display of fire, so of course we did not take her too far into it. But we stood quite close to the cart, from which the Archbishop (Fatty Lloyd) read the Bonfire Prayers, attended by his staff of clergy, all of whom we knew, and the Commander-in-Chief (Harry Cruse) a friend of ours. We had some fun there. Just after the Archbishop had denounced Pope Paul and had shouted "what shall we do with him Boys?" and they had shouted "Burn him! Burn him!" The tableau was seen to be alight, fired by some mischievous hand, before its turn. So they shouted "save the Pope, save the Pope", not as a sign that they had in any way relented their decision but because the tableau, once started, had to blaze away and a wonderful sight it was too.

I have seen 'set pieces' of fireworks at the Crystal Palace, but nothing like this! During the destruction, one could see the heads of Guy Fawkes and his confederates looking over the top and falling one by one, thus fulfilling the title of the structure 'Bold treason's fate is Tower Gate'. Then when the Pope was showing what good stuff he was made of, for burning, the crowd sang 'Rule Britannia' and afterwards, when all was destroyed, we sang 'God save our King'. Then we followed the procession until they dispersed and we returned once again to Hill Lodge earlier than the year before, and cleared away the supper and retired to bed about midnight.

This account was found by Mrs Kate Washer in an old notebook after the death of her mother Annette Pettitt nee Verrell. Annette left school aged twelve and became a parlourmaid at Hill Lodge, St Ann's Hill, Lewes.

******

Cliffe Bonfire Society members with banners taken at the rear of the Dorset Arms, Malling Street, Lewes during the Edwardian Era. This photo is on display at Anne of Cleves House, Southover High Street, Lewes.

Lewes Bonfire Society Information
By Brian W Pugh
(Correct as of October 2011)

Borough
Formed 1853
Pioneers
Smugglers
Fire site

Motto Death or Glory
HQ St. Mary's Supporters Club
Zulu Warriors
Blue & White
Landport Bottom, Nevill Road

Cliffe
Formed 1853
Pioneers
Smugglers
Fire site

Motto Nulli Secundus
HQ The Dorset Arms
Vikings
Black & White
Ham Lane

Commercial Square
Formed 1855
Pioneers
Smugglers
Fire site

Motto For Independence
HQ The Elephant & Castle
North American Indians
Black & Gold
Landport Recreation Ground

Nevill Juvenile
Formed 1967
Pioneers
Smugglers
Fire site

Motto We Dare
HQ St. Mary's Supporters Club
Medieval
Green & White
Landport Bottom, Nevill Road

South Street
Formed 1913
Pioneers
Smugglers
Fire site

Motto Faithful Unto Death
HQ Royal British Legion
Colonial Period (1750s)
Brown & Cream
Railway Lane

Southover Motto   Advance
Re-Formed 2005   HQ   The Kings Head
Pioneers   Priory Monks
Smugglers   Red & Black
Fire site   Stanley Turner Ground

Waterloo   Motto   True To Each Other
Re-formed 1964   HQ   The Lamb
Pioneers   Mongolian Empire
Smugglers   Red & White
Fire site   Brooks Road

******

Lewes Borough Bonfire Society Guy Fawkes 2007
(Courtesy of Donald McCrimmon)

A TIME LINE OF BONFIRE IN LEWES
1555 – 2010

1555 Between 1555 and 1557 there were 17 Protestant Martyrs that were burned at the stake in Lewes High Street outside The Star Inn (now the Town Hall). Those being: on 22nd July 1555 Dirick Carver (or Deryk or Diricke) of Brighton, 6th June 1556 Thomas Harland and John Oswald both of Woodmancote, Thomas Avington and Thomas Reed (or Read) both of Ardingly, about 20th June 1556 Thomas Wood (a Minister of the Gospel), Thomas Myles (or Mills) of Hellingly, 22nd June 1557 Richard Woodman, George Stevens both of Warbleton, Alexander Hosman (or Hosmar), William Mainard (or Maynard) and Thomasina Wood all of Mayfield, Margery Morris and her son James Morris both of Heathfield, Denis Burges (or Burgis) of Buxted, Ann Ashdon of Rotherfield and Mary Groves of Lewes.

1605 The Gunpowder Plot conspiracy to blow up the Houses of Parliament and King James I at the opening of Parliament. Guy (or Guido) Fawkes was arrested on the morning of 5th November 1605 in vault below the House of Lords; his fellow conspirators were Robert Catesby, Thomas and Robert Winter (also spelt Wintour), Thomas Percy (also spelt Piercy), John and Christopher Wright, Thomas Bates, Robert Keyes, Everard Digby, Ambrose Rookwood, Hugh Owen, John Grant (also spelt Graunt) and Francis Tresham.

Digby, Robert Winter, Grant and Bates were executed on 30 January 1606, Thomas Winter, Rookwood, Keyes and Fawkes were executed on

31 January 1606. Catesby, Percy, John and Christopher Wright were slain in the rebellion at Holbeach (also spelt Holbeache) House on 8 November 1605 and Francis Tresham died on 22 December 1605 at The Tower of London.

1606 Following the discovery of the Gunpowder Plot, an Act of Parliament 'For a public Thanksgiving to Almighty God every year on the 5th of November', required the ringing of the church bells and the conducting of a service in every parish church in England. The first anniversary of the discovery of the Gunpowder Plot, bonfires in all parts of the country were lit, including one on Cliffe Hill, not far from where the Martyrs' Memorial now stands.

1679 Following Titus Oates's 'exposure' of a Popish plot to kill the King, anti-catholic processions similar to those held in London were seen in Lewes on 5th. Carrying banners proclaiming the corruptions of the Roman Church, people attired in clerical regalia paraded an effigy of the Pope through the streets, finally late at night to committing it to flames. The first detailed description of the Lewes celebrations appeared in *The Domestick Intelligence* (No. 39) dated 18 November 1679, Benjamin Harris reported: Lewes in Sussex, Nov. 5. This day was celebrated with extraordinary solemnity, there being a procession not unworthy taking notice of. In the first place went a company of young men armed with swords and muskets, pikes &c. like a company of soldiers..." "Just before the Pope marched Guy Faux with his dark Lanthorn...", "...between twenty and thirty boys with vizards, and two or three who had their faces painted...," "...one whereof carried Holy Water in a tin pot, sprinkling the people with a bottle brush" ..."In this manner they having carried his Holiness through the Town and Streets..." "...they committed him to the flames..."

1688 On 5th November William, Prince of Orange landed at Brixham, Devon.

1723 An old churchwarden's account book has an entry as follows: 'Nov, ye 5th. Item: Pd. ye ringers being ye day of Deliverance from ye powder plott...2/6d."

1757 The town authorities paid two shillings for "giving notice about the Bonfire and watching the same".

1770 In the early 1770s street bonfires, squibbing and a general disorder were common practice with an established firesite at the top of School Hill.

1785 The Riot Act had been read and nine ringleaders sent to the House of Correction.

1795 The *Sussex Weekly Advertiser* of November 9th, reported a fire at the Star Inn, caused, it stated, 'by the indifference of some thoughtless persons who had amused themselves by letting off serpents and crackers in the great parlour of the Inn.'

1797 The Bonfire Boys, in face of opposition from the authorities, lit the bonfire regardless. The main Bonfire Boy had a dark lantern in one hand, a match in the other and a bundle of shavings hung across his shoulder, and singing "God Save the

King" he lit the bonfire.

1806 The Fifth was particular riotous with 18 Bonfire Boys arrested and the bonfire was moved to Castle Banks.

1808 The *Sussex Weekly Advertiser* of November 7th reported 'The Anniversary of Gunpowder Plot passed off here, on Saturday, in a very quiet and proper manner, the Boys made a bonfire in a very safe place, on the Castle Banks, and let off the crackers...'

1813 The diary of the late John Holman (High Constable of Lewes) gives us our first glimpse of things to come by the entry 'November 5th Gunpowder Plot observed by the boys, a fire on Gallows Bank, which passed off without any particular accident.'

1823 The site of the Bonfire was returned to the High Street outside the Star Inn (now the Town Hall).

1829 The celebrations took on a new character, the custom of dragging blazing tar barrels through the streets was introduced and the use of fireballs became common. Processions first introduced with a fire on Cliffe Hill, with the general rendezvous at Mount Caburn.

1831 In an effort to stop these dangerous practices of dragging blazing tar barrels through the streets, the magistrates issued cautions, but the 'boys' displayed even greater energy.

1832 Blazing tar barrels were rolled through the streets, an attempt to stop proceedings failed.

1834 Barrels were used to build a bonfire in the High Street outside the County Hall (now the Law Courts).

1838 Great rioting and several arrests were made with fines up to £15 imposed. A local magistrate, Mr Whitfield, JP, had a sharp encounter with some 'Bonfire Boys' on Cliffe Bridge (generally held to be the origin of the custom of throwing a blazing tar barrel into the river).

1839 The *Sussex Agricultural Express* of November 9th reported 'The celebration of the Popish Plot, although attended with usual "lettings off" and tar barrels dragged through the streets, was free from any serious accident or mischief. The inhabitants of the Cliffe lit up the Coombe with a blazing bonfire, which had a very pleasing effect in the distance. In Southover, the lieges were entertained with a merry peal on the bells, and in all other respects the day was observed with due regard to "Ancient Customs"'.

1841 Special constables were sworn in for another attempt to stop the celebrations on the 5th. The Bonfire Boys armed themselves, and Superintendent Flanigan (or Flanagan) and some of his men were roughly treated. At the following Assizes, more than twenty of the rioters were sent to prison for terms of up to two months.

1842 Proceedings were more orderly and bands were introduced for the first time. Tunes played included "Rule Britannia", "Rory O'More", See the Conquering Hero Comes" and "God Save the Queen".

1843 The *Sussex Express* stated that 'Since O'Connell and the Irish priesthood had denounced their fellow-subjects, the English as Saxon tyrants, the desire for celebrating the fifth of November in this town was increased among many of its respectable inhabitants.'

1845 In the Cliffe the parties were attended by a band and several banners, one with a death's head and marrowbones and another with **Tar-barrel Society**. The **Tar-Barrel Society** in the Cliffe area, probably only existed for one year.

1846 Another attempt was made to clear the 'Boys' from the streets which led to more rioting and another magistrate, Mr Blackman, J.P being seriously injured.

1847 One hundred and seventy of the principal tradesmen and other 'respectable inhabitants' were summoned to be sworn in as special constables. On their way to a meeting on the night of November 4th, they were attacked by Bonfire Boys in the High Street. Tar-barrels were lighted and several incidents occurred. The police fastened a chain across the road near Keere Street and ambushed some of the 'Boys', who were arrested. The next day 100 of the 'A' Division of the Metropolitan Constabulary arrived, and great was the excitement in Lewes that evening. It was an incident involving the mail-gig from Brighton which brought things to a head. Lord Chichester (or Earl of Chichester) read the Riot Act from the steps of the County Hall and gave the crowd five minutes in which to depart. In the free fight that ensued, many of the Metropolitan Police were injured, but the streets were eventually cleared.

1848 A committee of local tradesmen was, chaired by Benjamin Flint and arrangements were made to carry out the celebrations on the Wallands Fields. The Lewes Band led the procession of some 2,000 people from the White Hart Inn to the Wallands for the bonfire and fireworks.

1849 Following a procession from the White Hart Inn celebrations were again held on the Wallands including a bonfire, rockets, squibs, crackers, balloons, fire balls and tar barrels.

1850 Pope Pius IX re-established the Roman Catholic hierarchy in England; Cardinal Wiseman became the Archbishop of Westminster. This led the townspeople to allow the Bonfire Boys back in the streets, and two great bonfires were lighted, one in front of the County Hall and one in front of Cliffe Church.

1851 Bonfire Boys with blackened faces and ingenious disguises rolled tar barrels down School Hill into the Cliffe. At Cliffe Corner a grand bonfire was lit and a capital effigy of the Pope was burnt.

1853 Bonfire Boys organise themselves into processions. The first societies thus formed were those of the **Cliffe** and **Town** or **Lewes Bonfire Society**. **Cliffe** marched on the Fifth in South Street, Malling Street and Cliffe High Street as far as Cliffe Bridge complete with a Band and "No Popery" banner; they burnt a Pope and Guy Fawkes.

1855 The first record of a tar barrel being thrown into the River Ouse from Cliffe Bridge. **Commercial** was formed.

1856 A feature of the demonstrations introduced by the **Cliffe** was the 'Lord Bishop' who 'officiated.' He wore full clerical uniform and gave a 'sermon' before the effigies were burnt.

1857 First mention of Fraternal Greetings on Cliffe Bridge (the natural boundary dividing the two societies) between the **Cliffe** and the **Lewes Bonfire Societies**. The first recorded reference to Bonfire celebrations in Waterloo Place.

1858 **Commercial** commenced activities and **Lewes Bonfire Society** changed name to **Lewes Borough Bonfire Society**. **Cliffe** was unfortunate when one of its members 'made off with the money box.' He was commemorated the following year by being burnt in effigy along with the Pope. **Waterloo** was reported as being "out in great force" with large banners, processions, blazing tubs and torches, the burning of effigies and a very large fire. In the Cliffe area **A Rising Generation** consisted of about 50 boys aged 5 to 10 years was formed.

1859 The youthful "rising generation" were called the **Chapel Hill Bonfire Boys**. **Cliffe** burnt their first "enemy of bonfire", an effigy of the man who stole the money from the collection box in 1858. **Waterloo** disbanded soon after this years celebrations.

1861 Members of the Albert Theatre, Uckfield joined the **Cliffe** procession.

1862 On 7 November 1862 the *Standard* (London) reported that "Lewes again made itself notorious in celebration of the anniversary of Guy Fawkes, or Gunpowder Plot. From eight o'clock a.m. and throughout the day, large and numerous groups of men, boys, and women were parading the town, and impressing upon the townspeople the desirability of remembering the 5th of November, &c. Though the rain came down most freely throughout the day, the same seemed to have but little effect." It also reported the "The horse of a groom, in the employ of Mr. Charles Beard, of Lewes, took fright at some boys dressed as Guys, threw its rider, and seriously injured him, but under the treatment of Dr. Murrell it is hoped he will recover." The Fifth had a Garibaldian theme (**Cliffe, Borough** and **Commercial**) and the **Rising Generation** marched with **Cliffe** with their own Band and their own effigy of the Pope.

1863 The Bonfire Societies held a commemorative celebration on the marriage of the Prince of Wales. On 16 October 1863 the *Essex Standard* reported "The boys of Lewes are making active preparation for the customary grand display on the 5th of November" and that "A very large accession is expected from the Brighton branch..." The Lewes committee held on 7 October expressed horror adopted by the Czar of Russia for the suppression of the rights of the people of Poland. It was agreed at this meeting that the proceeds of the celebrations this year be sent to the Polish Relief Fund. **Borough** carried the monster iron key of the Borough for the first time. **The Rising Generation**, an enterprising party of youths in the Cliffe, celebrated the Fifth in a very appropriate manner by processions admirably got up.

1864 On 8 January 1864 saw the birth of Prince Albert Victor and there was great rejoicing all over the country including Lewes where the birth was celebrated by the ringing of Old Gabriel, the military and town band paraded the town. The *Standard* (London) on 12 January reported "In the evening a grand procession of the Lewes Bonfire Boys paraded the town with splendid bands, banners, &c., blue candles, and lights, returning to the County Hall, where "Rule Britannia" and "God save the Queen" were performed by the town and military bands, and at ten o'clock the old town was once more quite." On the 16 May (Whit Monday) the Bonfire Societies celebrated the 600th anniversary of the Battle of Lewes.

1866 **Commercial** were in financial difficulties but were saved by the **Sun Street Rising Generation** who took over the Commercial badges and banners and ran the celebrations for two years. **Cliffe** burnt an effigy of Pope Pius IX each year until 1878

1868 **Borough** introduced two new banners "Borough Bonfire Boys" and the society motto "Death or Glory". The **Sun Street Rising Generation** became **Commercial**.

1869 An effigy of Pope Pius IX exploded outside the Roman Catholic Chapel by **Borough**.

1870 It appears there was a **South Street Bonfire Society** in existence, probably for only one year. In January the Roman Catholic Church in Irelands Land was opened amid a disturbance involving the congregation, police officers and Bonfire Boys. In November **Cliffe** burnt an effigy of Archbishop Manning, and the Brighton Branch of the **Cliffe** joined the procession.

1871 *The Daily News* (London) on 22 November 1871 the news of "The Brighton Poisoning Case." Christina Edmunds was awaiting trial on several charges of distributing poison at Brighton. The report stated that "On the 6th November the "Lewes Bonfire Boys" – a society which is said, numbers over 1000 members and has the countenance and support of many gentlemen residing in the district – burnt an effigy of the prisoner in the public square of Lewes." Again from The *Daily News* (London) on 25 November 26 1871 there appeared a letter from "A Lewes Elector", saying "…in your impression of the 22nd instant refers to the "Lewes Bonfire Boys." …"there are several Bonfire Boys' Societies here," "By one of these, **Cliffe**, Miss Edmunds' effigy was burnt, not in the public square of Lewes, but in the Cliffe, a sort of suburb". **The Rising Generation of Southover** formed.

1872 **St. Michaels Bonfire Society** in existence probably for one year. The Crystal Palace Fireworks and gauze wire eye protectors first introduced by W. Banks (special agent to Messrs. C.T. Brock) 23 Station Street, Lewes. Reported in the *Leeds Mercury* on 7 November 1872 stated that "Lewes kept up the annual saturnalia" on 5 November. "There were men in armour, in clowns' dresses, equipped as Roman warriors, and flitting about in make-up of stage ghosts, with long, tailing, white bed-gowns, and full-frilled nightcaps, and with faces painted blue and green and crimson." "First came a great company of men and women dressed in ordinary costume,"..."walking eight abreast." This was followed by a band "playing a 'No Popery' tune,"...a great banner followed at least ten feet in height and extended across the street. "On it was inscribed 'Borough Bonfire Boys.'" Outside they pitched their bonfire outside County Hall in the High Street; the fire "...was as high as the closely adjoining shutter tops...its broad tongues of flames leapt as high as the first-floor windows." At St. Michael's Church there was another fire blazing. "This was where 'the Lord Bishop in full canonicals' was to deliver his protest against all things Papistical. The closing of his book was the signal for the destruction of Guy Fawkes." 1872 saw the pioneers first appearing in the **Cliffe** proceedings as a group of Chinese heading the procession.

1873 **Cliffe** had a friendly meeting with **Borough** on Cliffe Bridge.

1874 The *Morning Post* dated 30 October 1874 reported owing to the outbreak of "typhoid fever in Lewes that the Bonfire "boys" have decided not to hold their annual demonstration on Guy Fawke's day." On the Fifth **Cliffe** marched to Ringmer to join the Ringmer-green boys celebrations. The annual bonfire celebrations that were postponed on the fifth were held on 30 December 1874, The *Morning Post* dated 31 December 1874 reported "The annual bonfire demonstration"..."...took place last evening. The proceedings were much tamer than usual, although a large number of persons appeared attired in grotesque costumes, and the usual number of processions took place."

1875 The **Waterloo** reformed and was noted for its "excellent fife and drum band, formed from its own members". **Cliffe** burnt a tableau that featured for the first time a British politician by the name of Samuel Plimsoll.

1876 **St. Anne's** were formed. The first record of the **Waterloo** issuing a programme of its celebrations and they joined the Grand Procession. **Cliffe** moved their headquarters to the Swan Inn, Malling Street (probably the White Swan) and the Cliffe Volunteer Fire Brigade were Pioneers until 1882

1878 The *Graphic* dated 9 November reported on the celebration of the fifth "…When it has grown quite dark—at six o'clock, say—there is suddenly heard, as though started by some preconcerted signal, the sounds of brazen music, and from so many different parts of the town,"…"the banner bearers, foremost of which is one inscribed "No Popery,…in their midst two enormous effigies, the one of the Pope, the other of Guy Fawkes,…" At ten o'clock the Guys were burnt and the shame bishop read a parody of the church service. It appears that at different parts of the town four or five other fires blazing. **Cliffe** burnt an effigy of Pope Leo XIII each year until 1891.

1879 On 4th November a torchlight procession was organised by the Brighton Bonfire Society to celebrate the Royal visit to Brighton of the Duke and Duchess of Connaught, the **Borough**, **Commercial**, **Cliffe** and **Waterloo** Societies attended. **Waterloo** received commendation in the Sussex Express for its "excellent arrangements" on the fifth and the "able manner in which it carried out its demonstration." The Society's Tableau was reported as one of the principal attractions.

1880 Both **Waterloo** and **St. Anne's** disbanded after this year's celebration.

1881 June 22 the Cliffe area became part of the Borough of Lewes.

1882 **Cliffe** pioneers were an Indian Chief and his Warriors.

1886 There were friendly greetings again on Cliffe Bridge between **Cliffe** and **Borough**, the first time for 10 years. **The Rising Generation of Southover** became **Southover**.

1887 The Bonfire Societies celebrated Queen Victoria's Silver Jubilee. It appears that 1887 was a wet evening; *The Times* of 7 November 1887 reported that the celebrations were "...carried out with the customary zeal and activity. The **Cliffe** Society started soon after 5 o'clock, and had their run to the Cliffe corner..." "At half past 5 the **Lewes Borough** and the **Commercial Square** Societies entered upon their processions..." "The Borough boys lit the bonfire before the County Hall." "...Cliffe boys fulfilled the time-honoured custom of throwing a lighted tar barrel over the bridge at the bottom of School Hill..." "...amid a downpour of rain the whole of the societies amalgamated in a grand procession to the central fire at the County Hall, the proceedings coming to an end about midnight." The estimated people on the streets were about 13,000 and accidents were very few. **Cliffe Juvenile Society**, with nearly 100 members, held their own procession and burnt their own effigy of the Pope. The **Rising Generation of St. Anne's** was formed.

1890   **Cliffe** moved their headquarters to the Wheatsheaf Inn, South Street. The **Rising Generation of St. Anne's** became **St. Anne's**.

1891   **Cliffe** burnt an effigy of the Pope each year from now on.

1892   **Sun Street Bonfire Society** existed probably only for one year, as did **Toronto Terrace Bonfire Society**.

1893   The Bonfire Societies celebrated the marriage of the Duke of York and Princess May of Teck. The Reverend Richardson at Southover Church held the first Thanksgiving Service, this was held on the Sunday prior to the "Fifth" and was attended by members of all the Bonfire Societies in Lewes. **Cliffe** had two bonfires this year, one at Cliffe Corner and one at the Snowdrop Inn, South Street.

1895   **St. Anne's** disbanded and **Cliffe** had a Squad of Bengal Lacers as pioneers and moved their headquarters to the Dorset Arms, Malling Street.

1897   On 21 June the Bonfire Societies celebrated Queen Victoria's Diamond Jubilee. The Brighton Naval Volunteer Cruising Club joined the **Cliffe** procession for three years with their own band.

1898 **Cliffe's** pioneers became A Squad of Lady Lancers.

1900 A torch light procession took place in the town to celebrate the relief of Mafeking, later in the year a second procession organised by **Cliffe, Southover, Commercial** and **Borough** took place to celebrate the Queens birthday. On the "Fifth" **Cliffe** marched beyond Cliffe Bridge for the first time, going as far as Fitzroy Library.

1901 In May the Martyrs Memorial on Cliffe Hill was unveiled by the Countess of Portsmouth. **Borough, Cliffe, Southover** and **Commercial** all celebrated the fifth.

1902 On 2 August the societies organised a torch light procession to celebrate the coronation of the King Edward VII.

1904 A large fire at Dusart's, 84-85 High Street on 4 October showed the inhabitants the danger of fire, and consequently on 17 October the famous Lewes Rouser and Large Roman Candles were prohibited.

1905 The last bonfire and firework display was held in Lewes High Street on Monday 6 November (as featured on the cover and title page of this book). The Thanksgiving Service was transferred from Southover Church and held at the Jireh Chapel. This the last year the **Cliffe** fire site was held at Cliffe Corner with Bishops on the balcony over Mr. Bosher's shop.

1906 Fires in the Streets and the dragging of lighted tar barrels through the streets suppressed. 130 police were on duty in the town and many people were arrested including four leading Bonfire Boys. In the ensuing court case they were acquitted of instigating the forming of a bonfire in Commercial Square. Due to financial difficulties, **Borough** combined with **Commercial** to form **Commercial Square and Borough Amalgamated Bonfire Society**; this arrangement only lasted two years. **Southover** disbanded. **Cliffe** relocated their fire from Cliffe Corner to Malling Fields.

1907 Police escorted all processions but were not needed, **Cliffe** held their Bonfire Prayers at Cliffe Corner.

1908 **Cliffe** held a Southover Grand Procession for 2 years; the fire site was in a field at the bottom of Davey's Lane.

1909 On the 21 July **Borough** was reformed at the Brewers Arms Hotel, Lewes. **Commercial Square** reformed after a two year amalgamation with **Borough**.

1911 The **Cliffe's** pioneers were the British Army at the time of Waterloo. In June the Bonfire Societies celebrated the coronation of George V and Queen Mary.

1913 **St. John Star Bonfire Society** was in existence but probably for only one year. **South Street Juvenile Bonfire Society** formed by Tom Wheeler, the idea being to give the children an opportunity to enjoy the Lewes Bonfire Celebrations, they held a single procession and had a bonfire. **Cliffe's** firesite was on Cliffe Hill near the Martyrs memorial for this year only.

1914 Activities suspended during World War I, 1914-1918.

1918 On 20 November the societies organised a torch light procession in the town to celebrate Armistice Day.

1919 **Cliffe** resumed the demonstrations, the only Society in the town to do so. Their headquarters was the Dorset Arms and the fire site was on Malling Hill, no effigy of the Pope was burnt. Although **South Street** reformed but they did not celebrate the "Fifth", all of their surplus funds, after paying expenses, were donated to Lewes Victoria Hospital.

1920 **South Street** held three processions on the fifth and **Cliffe** again celebrated on their own, no effigy was burnt.

1921 **Borough** revived their celebrations; it had been suspended for 8 years, with their fire site being at the Ham off Southover High Street.

1922 **Commercial** reformed and held their bonfire at Landport. On the 4 November **Cliffe** laid a wreath and sounded "The Last Post" at the town's war memorial, their pioneers were Saxon Kings and Queens. The pioneer dress of **South Street** was Egyptians and the fire site was in front of Willie Cottages, South Street.

1923 **Southover** reformed and with **Borough** they used a common site for the destruction of their tableaux and effigies.

1924 **Cliffe** burnt an effigy of the Pope and the "No Popery" banner was carried, the first mention in a newspaper report of Sussex by the Sea being played in **Cliffe's** procession.

1925 Roman Gladiators were the **Cliffe** pioneers. The **South Street** fire site was now in the Chalkpit beside the headquarters The Snowdrop. King George V sent a personal message to the **Cliffe**

1926 **St. Anne's** reformed after a lapse of nearly 30 years.

1927 Photograph of **Borough** tableaux reproduced in the "New York Herald-Tribune". In the local press **South Street** were praised for their high standard of costumes and **Cliffe** were the only society to burn an effigy of the Pope.

1928 The **South Street** processions were joined by the recently re-established Ringmer Bonfire Society. **Cliffe** did not hurl the tar barrel into the River Ouse because of gas main repairs on Cliffe Bridge.

1929 Grecian costumes were now the pioneers of **South Street**. **Cliffe** joined the recently formed District Council of the Bonfire Societies in Lewes.

1930 **South Street** carried hand lights as well as torches in every procession. The first Combined Procession took place, led by **Cliffe** supported by **Borough**, **Commercial**, **Southover** and **St. Anne's** societies.

1931 **Cliffe** resigned from the Bonfire Council as the only Society maintaining the tradition of burning a papal effigy. The society then took no further part in the Combined Procession. The **Cliffe** pioneers were Indian Rajahs and Princes.

1932 Pioneers of **Cliffe** were Vikings. The Committee and members of **South Street** carried out all the bonfire preparations in just twelve weeks, including fund raising, and the total cost of the evening to the society was £32.

1933 **Cliffe** still carried out the true traditions despite great opposition and introduced the Scots as pioneers. **South Street** introduced Valencian costume as pioneers. There was no Combined Procession this year.

1934 **South Street** hurled a tar barrel in to the Ouse for the first time. A model of the Martyrs Memorial was carried in **Cliffe's** procession and the Martyrs Memorial on Cliffe Hill was floodlit on the Fifth for the first time.

1935 In May the Silver Jubilee of King George V and Queen Mary was celebrated with a grand procession with **Commercial**, **South Street**, **Cliffe**, **Southover**, **St. Anne's** and **Borough**. The display took place in a field off the Brighton Road opposite Houndean Rise. On 6 November 1935 *The Times* carried a report on the celebrations, the town were at the elections at time, but these were given up for the day. It reported "From early evening until midnight Lewes was all gaiety, pageantry, and fireworks. In other parts of the town marched gaily costumed processions. There were six of these. Each had bands, banners, and effigies of Guy Fawkes, Catesby, Hitler, and Mussolini, all of which were duly burnt." "Torches flared and crackers exploded everywhere. Among the latter were effective examples of the famous Lewes Rouser, which, it is claimed, produces "the biggest bang in the world." It explodes like a small cannon. Blazing tar barrels were hauled by some processions. That of the **Borough Society** was tipped into the Ouse by way of asserting a right that was challenged some years ago." "In the pyrotechnic displays some fine topical effects were introduced. One set-piece designed to convey the **Borough Society's** congratulations to the Duke of Gloucester and his Bride contained over 1,000 fireworks. As a grand finale the procession assembled in front of the County Hall, where the National Anthem and "Auld Lang Syne" were sung." At the end of the evening **Cliffe** held their Bonfire Prayers at Cliffe Corner with a small bonfire.

1936 **Borough** tableaux featured in the New York Tribune, and they burnt an effigy of Pope Paul V for the first time since the war. **Cliffe** were given permission by East Sussex County Council to suspend 3 banners across Cliffe High Street. **Commercial** was ignited fire prior to the fifth but were helped by other societies to build a new one.

1937 **Borough** programme for 1937 cost 6d and included admission to the bonfire and display in Smith Field, Ham Lane or to the Dripping Pan. **Commercial** held their fire near the Motor Road, probably near where Sheepfair is now, **South Street** changed their headquarters from the

Snowdrop Inn to The Thatched House and their celebrations on the fifth were filmed by British Paramount News. All the Bonfire Societies celebrated the coronation of King George VI at the Dripping Pan.

1938 **South Street** tableau was ignited prematurely by rockets thrown by the crowd. **Cliffe** shook hands with **Borough** on Cliffe Bridge on the fifth.

1939 Activities suspended during World War II, 1939-1945. **Southover** probably disbanded about this time. On the Sunday after bonfire night, members of **South Street** laid a wreath on the Town War Memorial after which they stood in silence to remember those who had fallen in the Great War, and those who were currently away fighting for King and Country. On 28 July at a meeting held at the Pelham Arms **St. Anne's** was disbanded due to the lack of interest.

1940 **South Street** members attended the annual service at the Jireh Chapel in Malling Street on the Sunday prior to the 5 November, and a wreath was laid on the Town War Memorial on bonfire day.

1945 On 9 May a torchlight procession was arranged by the Committee of Bonfire Societies to leave the Swan Inn to the War Memorial and then on to County Hall, this was to celebrate Victory in Europe (VE Day). On 16 August a combined procession of the Bonfire Societies marched around the town before ending up at a bonfire site at the top of Mill Road celebrating Victory over Japan (VJ Day). A meeting on 21st August at the Prince of Wales in Malling Street saw the **Cliffe**

move back into action with plans to celebrate the first post-WWII Fifth. W.H. Penfold (Banana Bill) was elected as chairman, W.R. Allen as secretary and S. Povey as treasurer. *The Times* of 5 November reported that Shoreham, after 45 years, revived its bonfire on Saturday 3 November 1945. "A large party of the Lewes "bonfire boys and girls," in traditional costume, headed a long torchlight procession." **Cliffe** received a personal message from King George VI. **Cliffe**, **Borough**, **Commercial** and **South Street** Bonfire Societies all resumed their celebrations. **Cliffe** marched to the War Memorial for the first time on the Fifth, an effigy of Pope Paul V was burnt at the fire site, the society featured in the American "Time" magazine that reported on the first bonfire after the war and Aubrey Taylor became Captain of Tar Barrels. **South Street** held their bonfire and firework display on the land behind the Thatched House public house in South Street.

1946   On 8th June the combined bonfire societies organised the victory over Europe celebrations, National Victory Day. The **South Street** Captain of Tableau was blown off the platform whilst clearing debris left by the tableau, he suffered burns and was taken to hospital and was allowed home after treatment. **Cliffe** held a procession to the Swan Inn, Southover.

1947   100th anniversary of reading of the Riot Act. Merlin Film Company filmed the Lewes proceedings on the fifth. As well as newsreel companies filming the celebrations, a film company, employed by the Central Office of Information, recorded the celebrations for inclusion in a feature "This is Britain". The film was exported overseas and shown in thirty-three Commonwealth Countries. **Borough** members visited the House of Commons and for the first time the "Bonfire Prayers" were recited on the spot.

1948 **Landport** formed mainly for the benefit of the children in the area, they held six processions on 5th November, a huge bonfire, firework display and the destruction of effigies of Guy Fawkes and Pope Paul V. The Lewes Bonfire Council (previously known as the Bonfire Societies Combined Committee) was formed by **Borough**, **Commercial**, **Landport** and **South Street** Bonfire Societies, **Cliffe** refused to rejoin from the Lewes Bonfire Council. First mention of the Zulus and Mexicans as pioneers appeared in the programme for **Borough**.

1949 The Zulus of **Borough** became the sole first pioneers and **Winterbourne** formed. **Landport** dispensed with the religious aspect and burnt effigies of Guy Fawkes and Robert Catesby, 4,000 torches were used in the procession that included a band, with **Cliffe** and **South Street** as visiting societies, the celebrations were held prior to bonfire night. **Cliffe** ignited a replica of the Martyrs Memorial outside the Town Hall.

1950 **Winterbourne** disbanded and reformed as **Southover**, they joined **Borough**, **Commercial** and **South Street** in one Grand Procession, with **South Street** leading. **Landport** held their celebrations prior to bonfire night, they were supported by **Southover** and **South Street**, some

4,800 torches and 100 hand lights were used in the processions. **Cliffe** did not join in the revamped United Grand Procession.

1951 On 15 September the Bonfire Societies took part in the Battle of Britain Week at Worthing. **South Street** pioneer changed to the Dutch national costume. During October **Landport** held their celebrations, they had three processions using 2,500 torches and on the 5th they joined the United Grand Procession. The United Grand Procession banned all mottoes of religious significance. Once again Lewes had steady rain all evening, (the wettest Fifth in living memory at the time) but it did not deter the Lewes Bonfire Society celebrating the 346th anniversary of the gunpowder plot. *The Times* of 6 November reported "The blazing tar barrel has been hurled into the river, the great bonfire has been set alight on Houndean Rise, there has been a brilliant display of fireworks, and the effigy of Guy Fawkes has been solemnly burned." The finale was outside the County Hall where the bonfire boys threw their torches onto a massive bonfire. The report closed "It has been a pleasant night, in spite of the rain, and it is all in aid of local charities."

In the same issue it stated the following: "The omission last night of the customary search of the vaults of the Houses of Parliament on the eve of a state opening of a new session, because the Sovereign will not be present, was given special point by the rare coincidence that this new session opens on the same date as that of 1605, on the eve of which Guy Fawkes was discovered with his barrels of gunpowder in the vaults."

1952 **Landport** once again took part in the United Grand Procession on the 5th but still held own celebration on a different night. They used 2,000 torches and had a special juvenile procession.

1953 On 25 May the Whit Monday Grand Carnival was held, organised by the Lewes Bonfire Society's. The Lewes societies organised a torchlight procession to celebrate the Coronation of Queen Elizabeth II. **Cliffe** the only bonfire society in the town with 100 years of independent existence, they ignited a replica of the Martyrs Memorial on Cliffe Bridge to the tune of "Land of Hope and Glory". **Borough** also celebrated their centenary. Because of shortage of funds **Landport** had to use a relay van to provide the music, nevertheless membership had increased and support was given by other Lewes societies.

1954 A blazing key is carried for the first time in the **Borough** procession also 1954 was the year that **Landport** used 3,000 torches in a display that cost £130, Lewes Town Band and Littlehampton Bonfire Society supported the processions. A BBC television unit filmed the proceedings on the fifth. **South Street** tableau was again ignited prematurely by rockets thrown by the crowd. **Cliffe** declined the invitation by the Lewes Bonfire Council to join the United Grand Procession. Loudspeakers were erected at Cliffe Corner with music and announcements about the times of the Society's processions and last trains from Lewes were relayed to the crowd. The procession route of **Cliffe** included Cliffe, Friars Walk, Station Street, School Hill and the Cliffe High Street.

1955 Walt Disney Productions filmed the proceedings in the town and **Borough** was the first society to have their fire and proceedings filmed. After a great deal of deliberation the **South Street** Committee finally decided to go ahead with their celebrations this year, but **Landport** disbanded.

1956 **South Street** changed their pioneer dress to Chinese.

1957 **South Street** used two bands in their processions for the first time.

1958 Bert Munt was made a life member of **Borough**, however he unfortunately passed away shortly afterwards. Broadcaster Gilbert Harding expresses a desire to 'dynamite' the town of Lewes on BBC's *What's My Line?* His effigy was duly blown up by **Cliffe**. This was the year that **Southover** disbanded.

1959 **South Street** torches were burnt a week before the fifth, but were replaced in time for the celebrations. **Cliffe** introduced badges for their officials designed by Ron Wright.

1960 Celebrations cancelled due to bad flooding in the town. However the wreaths were still placed on the War Memorial. On 19 November **South Street** carried out a modified programme but no processions with a display of effigies that were destroyed in the South Street chalk pit, on the Fifth **Borough** staged their celebrations at Chailey Heritage while **Cliffe** and **South Street** celebrated at Firle who held a traditional celebration.

1961 A private individual submitted a request to display a banner across Lewes High Street between St. Michael's Church and the County Hall bearing the words "Know Popery", consent was refused by East Sussex County Council, even though consent had been given to **Cliffe** to erect their "No Popery" Banner across Cliffe High Street. **Cliffe** member Bill Penfold was made the first Life Member. **Cliffe** had no collection boxes this year as they had been so well supported.

1962 **Waterloo Place Bonfire Society** existed for two years. Because the East Sussex County Council refused to grant consent to the **Cliffe** to erect their "No Popery" banner across Cliffe High Street, it was attached to the front of a premises on the corner of Malling Street and Chapel Hill.

1963 A dart match between **Cliffe** and **Borough** held at the Dorset Arms resulted in 5-4 win for **Cliffe**. Golden Anniversary of **South Street**.

1964 On 9 May **Cliffe** took an active part in the town celebrations to mark the 700th anniversary of the Battle of Lewes; **Borough**, **Commercial** and **South Street** also took part. **Borough** took a leading role in the Battle of Lewes celebrations and was solely responsible for the illumination of Cliffe Hill. 1964 was also year that **Waterloo** was reformed, there were four processions accompanied by Banana Bill's car with a loud speaker attached to the roof playing marching band music. The **Lynchets Bonfire Society** existed for probably only one year.

1965 There was no combined procession for the first

time for 15 years, **South Street** combined with **Commercial** for one procession. A band was introduced to the **Waterloo** processions and 1,000 torches were made. **Cliffe** "No Popery" banner was hung but was taken down by officials and members as the processions were about to start.

1966 **Cliffe** contributed part of its charity collection to the Mayor's flood relief fund and the sum of £10 10s (£10.50) to the Aberfan Relief Fund; they gave a special firework display for the children at the Chailey Heritage School. Still no combined procession so **Borough** combined with **Commercial** for one procession and **South Street** combined with **Cliffe** also for one procession, to and from the War Memorial. Two bands paraded with **Waterloo**. **Cliffe's** "No Popery" banner was hung and then taken down and hung across a café in Cliffe Square.

1967 On 9 September **Cliffe** and **South Street** supported the Woodingdean Carnival. 1967 was the year that the celebrations were marred by the floods. Only the peak of the **Waterloo** bonfire was visible (at the Pells) and they joined the United Grand procession for the first time. **Borough** celebrations were recorded by Mr Bob Danvers-Walker on BBC Radio Four. Philip Amey and Peter Earl held the first proceedings of **Nevill**, one procession marched around the allotments, they had 50 torches and 40 people attended, and there was a fire and fireworks, a small set piece was made by Charlie Earl and so **Nevill** was formed. **South Street** marched alone even though there was a United Grand Procession.

1968 On 13 July **Cliffe** took part in the Lewes Carnival. On 9th November **Nevill** held their first processions, with 7 processions, 600 torches and 70 members, on the Nevill Estate. On 17th December **Nevill** committee was formed with separate captains for Effigies and Tableaux, the Chairman Peter Earl, Vice-Chairman Philip Amey and the Secretary being Wendy Earl. **South Street** rejoined the United Grand Procession and during the year entertained the children at Chailey Heritage. **Waterloo** led the United Grand Procession.

1969 **Waterloo** was praised for their new pioneer front representing the costumes of the savage tartar of the Genghis Khan. East Sussex County Council still said no to the **Cliffe** "No Popery" banner hanging in Cliffe High Street, prompting a popular tableau entitled Gunpowder Plot 1969, criticising the County Council's new £21 million headquarters in the town. United Grand was the longest ever. **Nevill** used 1,500 torches in four processions, their pioneers were Apache Indians and **Borough** joined them for the evening. **South Street** changed their Pioneers to Siamese Dancers and again entertained the children at Chailey Heritage.

1970 In the early 1970s **Cliffe** march up and down South Street for the last time. **Nevill** first fund raising event, a jumble sale raised £29, they now had 160 members and Peter Earl resigned as Chairman, the Pioneers were changed from Apache Indian to Cossack Dancers. The **Cliffe** "No Popery" banner is permitted to be hung again. And 1970 saw Fred Playford being made the first life member of

Waterloo. **South Street** joined the United Grand.

1971 **Commercial** amalgamated with **Borough** at the fire held on the Landport Estate. **Nevill** introduced as Cossacks as pioneer and membership reached 200, they were joined in their celebrations for the first time by **Waterloo**. **South Street** led the United Grand Procession and were filmed by Southern ITV. The **Cliffe's** headquarters was The Kings Head in Southover, the pioneers were Cavaliers and the society took part in Lewes Bonfire Fancy Dress Competition that was held for the first time since 1957.

1972 On 8 July Lewes Carnival was held in which **Cliffe** took part. **Cliffe** rejoined the Bonfire Council, but continues to march alone; they were allowed two banners to be suspended in Cliffe High Street. **Cliffe** members awake on the morning of the Fifth to discover that the fire had been torched overnight; by that evening an arguably larger one was ready for the celebrations. **Nevill** joined the Lewes Bonfire Council and society membership reached nearly 300. **South Street** membership reached over 280.

1973 **Cliffe** visited Europe; the Society took part in celebrations in the twin town of Blois, France. The **Borough** motto 'Death or Glory' was re-introduced into the procession and the first torch lit procession in Europe - Blois, France took place, **Nevill** also took part. A torch light procession took place in Brighton with **Borough**, **Commercial**, **Cliffe**, **South Street** and **Nevill** taking part. Frimley and Camberley Carnival was held on 30 June with **Commercial**, **Borough**, **Cliffe**, **South**

Street, **Waterloo** and **Nevill** attending the torch light procession. On the 5th November, a CS gas canister was discharged at the **Cliffe** fire site at Malling Hill, resulting in 15 people being rushed to hospital, the culprit was never found. At the **Cliffe** Christmas Dinner held on 24 November in a reply to the claim by **Borough** that they are the oldest society, Ron Wright, Chairman of the society, stated 'that in 1853 two societies were formed, **Lewes Town** and **Cliffe**. In 1859 Town changed their name to **Borough**; between 1906 and 1908 they disappeared and went under the war bonnets of **Commercial**'. **South Street** celebrated their 60th anniversary.

1974 On 29 June the Bonfire Societies stage a Pageant of Bonfire History held at the Dripping Pan as part of the Festival of Lewes, the inter-society blazing tar barrel race was won by **South Street**. **Nevill** played a large part in Pageant. They also introduced firework banners into the processions on the fifth, and the society's celebrations and preparations, as was **Cliffe**, were filmed by Central London Polytechnic, this was partly sponsored by **Cliffe** and **Nevill**. On New Year's Eve a torchlight procession took place from Cliffe Corner to Southover Grange to commemorate the occasion 100 years before when the celebrations were delayed by a typhoid epidemic, this organised by **Cliffe**, with **Nevill, Commercial** and **South Street** attending. **Cliffe** reintroduced the men's barrel run in Cliffe High Street.

1975 **Nevill** changed their pioneers to Samurai Warriors and Japanese Ladies. On 17 October **Cliffe** and **Nevill** presented a showing of the film 'Bonfire' at the Town Hall; this was filmed during the 1974 celebrations. **Cliffe** pioneers were Vikings. **South Street** had the longest procession in Lewes on the Fifth with over 200 members and 7 visiting societies.

1976 On 15 May the Lewes Pageant was held at the Convent Field, members of **Cliffe** and **South Street** took part. **Nevill** marched with **Cliffe** on the fifth. **Cliffe** enemies of bonfire became a regular feature. Tom Wheeler was made first life member of **South Street**, and Bill Penfold (Banana Bill) long time **Cliffe** member passed away. On Cliffe Bridge **Cliffe** and **Borough** exchanged fraternal greetings.

1977 On 6 June for the Queen's Silver Jubilee **Borough** led Her Majesty the Queen to light her Jubilee Beacon in the Great Park at Windsor, with societies from Newhaven, Crowborough, Rotherfield and Mark Cross, Mayfield, Shoreham, Seaford, Buxted, Burgess Hill, Uckfield, Littlehampton, East Hoathly and Halland. The Lewes Bonfire Council and the town's societies, except **Borough**, organised a torch light procession through the town of Lewes to the Grand Fireworks display at Malling Brooks to mark the Queen's Silver Jubilee on 6 June. 10th Anniversary of **Nevill**, they marched with **Waterloo** on the fifth and **Landport** was reformed with their procession was supported Portslade Girl Pipe Band, **Borough**, **Cliffe**, **Commercial**, **Nevill**, **South Street** and **Waterloo**. Tom Wheeler the founding member of **South Street** passed away.

1978 Full-scale live television coverage took place by

the BBC – some television coverage in most subsequent years. **Waterloo** acted as hosts to the BBC, the firework display was televised to the nation and the Society engaged their first military band. **Nevill** introduced a printed programme for the first time and **South Street** made a final donation to purchase a Guide Dog for a blind person.

1979 **Cliffe** took part in 'Leisure in Lewes' exhibition by displaying costumes, tar barrels and other regalia. **Landport** disbanded. 'Carols for the Queen', on 16 December **Borough** led a torch light procession from Horse Guards to Buckingham Palace, the procession consisted of Newhaven, Herstmonceux, Chanctonbury Morris Dancers, Littlehampton, Clapham and Patching, Seaford, Uckfield, Rotherfield and Mark Cross, Buxted, East Hoathly and Halland, Crowborough, Rye, Burgess Hill, Edenbridge, Cliffe, Waterloo, Newick, South Street, Commercial, Fletching and Landport. The Queen listened to the carols from the balcony of Buckingham Palace to mark the end of International Year of the Child.

1980 **Cliffe** leased some land and built its own workshops and storage facilities in Ham Lane. Adverse publicity concerning the burning of the Effigy of Pope Paul V forces Ministry of Defence to ban Military Bands from **Cliffe** processions, Vikings were the pioneers. The **Nevill** tableau was a full size replica of Stevenson's Rocket, manoeuvred along 200 foot track.

1981 The Bonfire Societies stage a firework display for the Lewes Mayoral centenary. On 17 September

20 members from each society in costume attended the "Lichfield Most Beautiful Women" dinner and ball at Grosvenor House Hotel, Park Lane, London, Princess Alexandra and the Hon. Angus Ogilvy were present. They provided a colourful back drop for the opening of the dinner. Mr Edward (Ted) Over, one of Lewes' much loved Bonfire Boys and member of **Borough** died following illness that prevented him from attending the bonfire celebrations for the first time in thirty five years, he had been Pioneer Chief and Treasurer of the Society. **Waterloo** moved their headquarters to the Crown Hotel (now the Crown Inn). Newhaven Youth Marching Band marched with the **Nevill** for the first time. The Reverend Ian Paisley was in Lewes to watch the celebrations.

1982   The fire site used in 1981 by **South Street** was unavailable this year due to work on the River Ouse banks so the society arranged to use the former British Rail Goods Yard off Railway Lane for their display. The **Commercial** fire was ignited prior to the fifth. **Cliffe's** procession included a Viking Long Boat.

1983   **Waterloo** changed its fire field after many years from the Pells to the Malling Brooks. And **Cliffe** successfully applied to the Registry of Friendly Societies to become Cliffe Bonfire Society Limited, Smugglers led the first Cliffe procession to celebrate the society's 130th year. An estimated crowd of 50,000 attended the celebrations.

1984   Michael Stevenson made the first life member of **Nevill**. Cavaliers and Roundheads were the pioneers of **Cliffe** for two years and there were no enemies of bonfire. **South Street** changed their pioneers to English Civil War.

1985 **Southover** reformed, and **South Street** were filmed at their fire site by the BBC and was featured on television. The **Waterloo** fire was ignited prior to the fifth. The Market Tower suffered damage at the end of the Fifth, both **Cliffe** and **Waterloo** denied responsibility.

1986 **Borough** and **Waterloo** took part in the Opening Ceremony of the Special Olympics held at the Withdean Stadium, Brighton. **Borough** were filmed on the 5th for German television. **South Street** did not take part in the fancy dress competition claiming 'unfair competition'. **Cliffe** pioneers were Vikings and **Nevill** pioneers were Valencians.

1987 **South Street** members joined a special train from Lewes to London to take part in the centenary celebrations of the St. John Ambulance Brigade. **Cliffe** held their last bonfire and display at the Mill Road fire site.

1988 The societies took part in a traditional German carnival at Waldshut-Tiengen. The Lewes Societies staged a firework display on the battlements of Lewes Castle to celebrate anniversary of Spanish Armada. And after nearly 40 years at their Mill Road fire site, **Cliffe** was forced to find a new temporary site at Brooks Road, Lewes. **South Street** celebrated their 75th Anniversary. An estimated crowd of 70,000 attended the celebrations.

1989 **Borough** suffered the sad loss of their President, Dr Pat Nicholl, they did not enter the fancy dress competition due to lack of interest. **Cliffe** once more moved its fire site to the outskirts of the town at Ham Lane where they burnt an effigy of the Archbishop of Canterbury. Mr Bob Allen, a Life Member since 1969, and Secretary of **Cliffe** for 25 years, passed away in December. **Southover** disbanded, and **Waterloo** celebrated their 25th anniversary.

1990 **Cliffe** charged £2.00 admission to the fire site for the first time. **Waterloo** held a superb firework display - The finest ever seen on bonfire night "This was our finest hour", they claimed. **South Street** travelled to Shoreham to help with fund raising for their new Lifeboat.

1991 **Cliffe** held the first Ladies' Barrel Race that took place from Cliffe Corner to Cliffe Bridge. **Waterloo** had a new banner presented to the Ladies of the Society by the treasurer John Armitage. The proposed road management structure created a major rift between the Bonfire Boys, Lewes District Council and the Emergency Services, when meetings held to discuss safety arrangements for the 5th saw the Bonfire Boys excluded. The Bonfire Boys stood firm, a meeting two weeks before the 5th with Local Police, healed the rift and the evening went ahead without problems. Some local councillors ended up being seen in a very poor light. **Nevill** introduced a new Grand Procession route including the full length of Nevill Road and Hawkenbury Way, and a glossy format programme was introduced. An estimated crowd of 55,000 attended the celebrations.

1992 A secret meeting takes place between Lewes District Council and Sussex Police resulting in new 'rules' to ban, among other things, under-16's carrying torches and marchers being closer than ten feet to each other. The resulting furore from Bonfire societies and the general public causes the ruling Lib Dem council to narrowly survive a vote of no confidence by 20 votes to 18 with three abstentions. If enforced it would have stopped the traditions that make Lewes Bonfire unique. The societies are eventually invited to contribute to the discussions and a Lewes Bonfire Safety Group is formed. **Nevill** celebrated their Silver Jubilee; the programme included black and white photographs for the first time. An estimated crowd of 60,000 attended the celebrations. **Cliffe** had 6 Enemies of Bonfire.

1993 End of **Nevill** narrowly averted by the appointment of a new committee. The **South Street Juvenile Bonfire Society** members decided to change their name to **South Street Bonfire Society**. An estimated crowd of 70,000 attended the celebrations.

1994 Mr John Brooks 'Lord Bishop of the **Borough**' celebrated thirty years service. The **Waterloo's** "Guido Fawkes" made his first appearance in the street. **Cliffe** appointed a safety officer for the first time. An estimated crowd of 80,000 attended the celebrations.

1995 **Cliffe** introduced the Cliffe Volunteer Fire Brigade with a replica of the fire engine and there were no enemies of bonfire.

1996 **South Street** withdrew from membership of the Bonfire Council, because Council Members were attending the Bonfire Safety Group meetings, to the detriment of the Lewes Bonfire Societies, therefore **South Street** did not enter the fancy dress competition or join the grand procession

1997 **South Street** rejoined the Bonfire Council; also this year saw the wettest Fifth since 1951 but Bonfire Boys and Girls carry on regardless despite thousands of spectators leaving the town early. The new Catholic parish priest, Father Flood, wryly denied any involvement!

1998 A splendid new banner depicting the 'Olde Borough Bonfire Boys' was proudly carried for the first time in the **Borough** processions. Due to the large crowd numbers meant that **Cliffe** made their fire site ticket only, priced at £3. **Nevill** introduced a Junior Tableaux team, heavy rain and high winds cause celebrations to be postponed for the first time and rearranged for three weeks later, where over 2000 people watched the display.

1999 Renovation work on a house in 51 South Street unearths a very old **South Street** banner. Research by the society indicated that the banner was created in the early 1920's. **Cliffe** had no enemies of bonfire.

2000 On 1st January the Lewes Bonfire societies and East Hoathly & Halland Carnival Society organised a Millennium Firework Display held at Malling Brooks, a spectacular 15ft high tableau of Old Father Time was the centre piece. In October flood devastates the town, **Cliffe** was forced to abandon its fire site only a week before and temporarily move to the Convent Field. **Waterloo** introduced four new banners, including the splendid new Millennium banner. Severe flooding of properties in South Street, Malling Street and Cliffe area. The **South Street** fire site at the former British Rail Goods Yard off of Railway Lane was unusable so the society made special plans to discharge their fireworks on the streets and "spare" land. The smallest number of visitors for decades, 10,000-15,000.

2001 Mr Eric Winter, life member and former President and Chairman of **Borough** passed away following illness. A new pioneer, Medieval, was introduced by **Nevill**, and the position of Safety Officer; the society now had more than 350 members. **South Street** travelled to Deal in East Kent to join, as the main attraction, their Street processions, the torches were transported to Deal and dipped on site. On the fifth an estimated 30,000 spectators attended. **Cliffe** bought the land at the Ham Lane workshop site.

2002 **Waterloo** celebrated the Queen's Golden jubilee in style by introducing the splendid "Jubilee" and the "God Save The Queen" banners. An estimated 25,000 spectators attended the celebrations.

2003 **Borough** celebrated its 150th Anniversary. **Cliffe** celebrated its sesquicentenary, the only Bonfire Society in the world with 150 years of uninterrupted existence. After years of fund-raising and searching, **Cliffe** also celebrated the purchase of its own fire site at Malling. For one year only the traditional 'Guernsey' (smugglers) formed the **Cliffe** pioneers, there no enemies of bonfire and a non-controversial tableau featuring a huge skull and crossbones wearing a smugglers red hat was ignited. **Nevill** required four bands for the longer processions and **South Street** returned to using the traditional materials of "tow" for their torches. It was estimated 35,000 spectators attended the celebrations. **Commercial** held the first "Proms in the Park" evening at The Paddock.

2004   Replica of Martyrs Memorial joined the **Nevill** procession for the first time, and 12 visiting Bonfire Societies attended, creating a procession of 600 marchers. Vikings returned as pioneers of **Cliffe**. It was estimated 45,000 attended the celebrations on the fifth.

2005   On the 8 May **Cliffe** celebrated the 60th anniversary of VE Day with a party at the Dorset Arms and on 22 July they commemorated the 450th anniversary of the martyrs execution with a small procession from the Town Hall to the Martyrs Memorial where they laid a wreath and exploded 17 maroons. At the **Cliffe** AGM Aubrey Taylor resigned as Captain of Tar Barrels after 60 years in the post, Malcolm Bassett was elected as Captain of Tar Barrels. On 16 September **Commercial** celebrated their 150th birthday and held a one day exhibition at the Corn Exchange of their costumes and archives. On 1 October **Cliffe** also held a one day exhibition at Southover Grange entitled 'Cliffe Uncovered' and displayed costumes, photographs and memorabilia. **Waterloo** celebrated the 400th anniversary of the discovery of the gunpowder plot. The band of the Brigade of Ghurkhas received a tremendous reception on their first visit to Lewes with **Waterloo**. **Borough** celebrated with a fantastic display of costumes and a record breaking forty foot effigy of Guy Fawkes. As guests of Mr Norman Baker MP for Lewes, members of **Borough** and **Commercial** visited the House of Commons and for only the second time Bonfire Prayers were recited within the walls. **Southover** was reformed and joined the united grand procession. To celebrate the 400th anniversary of the discovery of the gunpowder plot, **South Street** made significant changes to their celebrations including additional fire banners, firework units and an A4 size programme. It was estimated that 65,000 spectators attended the celebrations.

2006 **Waterloo** moved their headquarters after 25 years from the Crown to the Lamb. Charlie Earl, **Nevill** and **Cliffe** member passed away. Accommodation to construct the **South Street** tableau etc. was a great problem which was only partially solved. It was estimated that 50,000 spectators attended the celebrations. In the Cliffe procession the Vikings marched with their new Viking Ship "Ravensclaw".

2007 David Quinn retired as the **Waterloo** Chairman after 27 years in office. David is acknowledged by the Society as the most influential person in achieving the Society's success, and **Nevill** celebrated its 40th Anniversary. Late payment of membership fees caused a cash flow problem for **South Street**, however a "gee-up" letter brought membership applications flooding in and the cash levels were reached. **Southover** held their fire at Cockshut Road for the first time.

2008 The Ghurkha's danced the Khukuri Dance for the first time for **Waterloo** at the War Memorial and **South Street** created a society own web-site. It was estimated that 50,000 spectators attended the celebrations.

2009 Mr. John Armitage retired as the **Waterloo** Treasurer after 29 years in office. **South Street** employed the services of a Samba Band and Dancers to accompany their processions. A new road closure scheme was introduced, main roads into the town were closed to traffic from 5pm and this caused problems for residents getting back to their homes.

2010 An estimated 40,000 attended the celebrations; there were no Enemies of Bonfire with **Cliffe** this year. **Borough** carried banners alleging a miscarriage of justice over the imprisonment of Martin and Nathan Winter who were found guilty of "gross negligence" following a massive explosion at a fireworks factory at Marlie Farm, Shortgate in December 2006 when two firemen died. **Borough** later offered an unreserved apology for any distress that was caused. The **Waterloo** tableau celebrated 100 years of Lewes Victoria Hospital. **Cliffe** and **Southover** both featured Nick Clegg (as David Cameron's puppet and as a human cannonball respectively). **Commercial** and **South Street** referred to the BP oil crisis in the Gulf of Mexico.

LEWES BONFIRE FANCY DRESS COMPETITION

All the winners' names are taken from the cups.

	Pioneer Cup	Points Cup
1948		Borough
1949	Commercial	Commercial
1950	Cliffe	Commercial
1951	Cliffe	Commercial/Cliffe (*)
1952	Commercial	Cliffe
1953	Commercial	Borough
1954	Commercial	Borough
1955	Commercial	Borough
1956	Borough	Borough
1957	Borough	Borough

The competition was not held again until 1971

1971	Borough	Borough
1972	Borough	Borough
1973	Borough	Cliffe
1974	Borough	Commercial
1975	Commercial	Waterloo
1976	Cliffe	Waterloo
1977	Commercial	Cliffe/Waterloo (*)
1978	Borough	Commercial
1979	Borough	Cliffe
1980	Commercial	Commercial
1981	Cliffe	Cliffe
1982	Cliffe	Cliffe
1983	Cliffe	Cliffe
1984	Borough	Waterloo
1985	Waterloo	Cliffe
1986	Cliffe/Commercial (*)	Cliffe
1987	Cliffe	Cliffe
1988	Cliffe	Waterloo

1989	Cliffe	Cliffe
1990	Cliffe	Cliffe
1991	Commercial	Cliffe
1992	Cliffe/Commercial (*)	Cliffe
1993	Borough	Cliffe
1994	Commercial	Waterloo
1995	Cliffe	Cliffe
1996	Commercial	Waterloo
1997	Borough	Waterloo
1998	Cliffe	Waterloo
1999	South Street	Waterloo
2000	Cancelled owing to floods, held 22 February 2001	
2001	Commercial	Borough
2001	Commercial	Borough
2002	Borough	Borough
2003	Borough	Borough
2004	Borough	Cliffe
2005	Borough	Cliffe
2006	Borough	Cliffe
2007	Cliffe	Cliffe
2008	Cliffe	Cliffe
2009	Commercial	Cliffe
2010	Borough	Borough

(*) = Tied result

Pioneer dress:
Commercial Square   Red Indians   Cliffe   Vikings
Borough   Zulus   Waterloo   Genghis Khan
South Street   English Civil War

There does appear to some differences in the following results:

1977
The programme for the 1978 Fancy Dress Competition

lists the 1977 winners and shows that Cliffe won the Pioneer Cup, whereas the cup shows Commercial.

1980

A newspaper reports Cliffe winning the Points Cup; whereas the cup shows Commercial as winners.

1981

A newspaper reports Cliffe and Commercial jointly won the Points Cup, whereas the cup shows Cliffe as winners.

1992

A newspaper reports Cliffe won the Pioneer Cup; whereas the cup shows joint winners Cliffe and Commercial.

1997

A newspaper reports Borough and Cliffe jointly won the Pioneer Cup; whereas the cup shows Borough as winners.

******

An early tar barrel that survived the celebrations.
(Courtesy of Brigid Chapman)

BONFIRE SOCIETIES IN LEWES 1845-to date

The years given are the first and last celebrations held by the societies.

Borough	1853-1905,
	1909-1913,
	1921-1938,
	1945-
Cliffe	1853-1913,
	1919-1938,
	1945-
Cliffe Juvenile	1887-1888.
Cliffe Square Bonfire Boys	c.1934.
Commercial Square & Borough B.S. (amalgamated)	
	1906-1908.
Commercial Square	1855-1866,
	1868-1905,
	1909-1913,
	1922-1938,
	1945-
Landport	1948-1954,
	1977-1979
Lynchets	1964.
Nevill Juvenile	1967-
Rising Generation of Chapel Hill	1859,
	1862-1863.
Rising Generation of Southover	1871-1885.
Rising Generation of St. Anne's	1887-1889.
Rising Generation of Sun Street	1866-1867.
(Also known as Rising Generation of Commercial Sq.)	
South Street Juvenile	1913,
	1919-1938,
	1945-1992.
South Street	1870.
South Street	1993-

Southover	1886-1906, 1923-1938, 1950-1958, 1985-1989, 2005-
St. Anne's	1876-1880, 1890-1895, 1926-1938.
St. John Star	1913.
St. Michaels	1872.
Sun Street Juveniles	1892.
Tar-Barrel Society (Cliffe area)	1845.
Toronto Terrace Boys	1892.
Waterloo Place	1962.
Waterloo	1857-1859, 1875-1880, 1964-
Winterbourne	1949.

1874	Typhoid epidemic in Lewes, celebrations cancelled in November, but were held in December.
1914-1918	First World War, no celebrations
1939-1944	Second World War, no celebrations
1960	The Flood Year, no celebrations

******

Research for the following lists is very limited, so the years of a society forming, disbanding etc. are very patchy and are shown as ???

List of Other Bonfire Societies

Existing Societies

Alford Bonfire Society (Surrey) c.2007-to date.
Barcombe Bonfire Society 1932-37, 1978-to date.
Battel Bonfire Boyes 1686-1906, 1911-to date.
Brighton Bonfire Society 2005-to date.
Brockham Bonfire Society (Surrey) 1606, late 1800s-to date.
Burgess Hill Bonfire Society c.1894-???, c.1900-???, 1969-to date.
Burwash Bonfire Society ???-to date.
Center For Fawkesian Pursuits Bonfire Society, Baltimore (the first bonfire society in North America) 1993-to date.
Chailey Bonfire Society 1996-to date.
Crowborough Bonfire & Carnival Society 1897-1913, 1948-to date.
Cuckfield Bonfire c.1874-c.1881, c.1985-to date.
East Dean and Friston Bonfire Society 1952-to date.
East Hoathly & Halland Bonfire & Carnival Society 1919-to date.
Eastbourne Bonfire Society 2001-to date.
Edenbridge Bonfire Society (Kent) 1928-to date.
Ewhurst & Staplecross Bonfire Society c.1930s/40s-to date.
Firle Bonfire Society c1879-1970s, 1981-to date.
Five Ashes Bonfire Society 2000-to date.
Fletching Bonfire Society 1854-1914, 1920-1939 (1947 British Legion), 1951-to date.
Hailsham Bonfire Society ???-1950s, 1980-1991, 2005-to date.
Hastings Borough Bonfire Society 1860-1945, 1995-to date.
High Hurstwood 1964-to date.
Isfield and Little Horsted Bonfire Society 2009-to date.

Lindfield Bonfire Society 1887-???, 1894-???, 1930-to date.
Littlehampton Bonfire Society 1952-to date.
Maresfield Bonfire Society 2003-to date.
Mayfield Bonfire Boyes & Belles 1556-???, 1935-to date.
Newick Bonfire Society reformed c.1887-???, 1937-to date.
Ninfield c.1888-???, 1940-1947, 2009-to date.
Ore Bonfire Society 2008-to date.
Phoenix Walking Group 2011.
Robertsbridge Bonfire Society 1895-1906, 1938-1940s, 1990-to date.
Robin Hood Bonfire Society (Icklesham) 1997-to date.
Rotherfield & Mark Cross Bonfire Society 1970-to date.
Rusthall Bonfire Appreciation Society (Kent) c.1978-to date.
Rye & District Bonfire Society 1695-???, 1880s-1930s, 1950s-1986, 1993-to date.
Seaford Bonfire Society c.1867-1938, 1972-1977, 2010-to date.
Selsey Community Bonfire Society 1979-to date.
Shoreham-by-Sea Bonfire Society 2009-to date.
South Heighton Bonfire Society 2002-to date.
Storrington Bonfire Society. ???-to date?
The Merrie Harriers (Herstmonceux) c.1960-to date.
Titchfield Bonfire Boys Society (Hampshire) 1880-1913, 1919-1938, 1946-to date.
Uckfield Bonfire & Carnival Society c.1827-to date.
Warbleton & Rushlake Green Bonfire Society 1996-to date.
Whatlington Renegades 1986-to date.
Who The Devil Are We? 2001-to date.
Winchelsea 1889-???, 1996-to date.
Winchelsea Beach Bonfire Society ???-to date.

Previous Bonfire Societies

Adversane Bonfire Society.
Arundel Bonfire Boys Society 1870s, 1800s, 1890s.
Battle Hill Bonfire Boyes 1907-1910.
Beckley 1930s.
Beeding & Bramber Bonfire Association 1940s/1950s.
Bexhill Bonfire Society 1888 [probably also known as the Castle Bonfire Society].
Billingshurst Guy Fawkes Club 1950s, 1955/1970?
Birdham Bonfire Club.
Blacksmiths Arms Bonfire Society (Newhaven) 1854.
Bognor Regis Bonfire Society 1880s-1906, 1950, 1990.
Bohemia Bonfire Boys (Hastings) 1900.
Brighton Borough Bonfire Society 2005-???
Brighton Bonfire Boys c. late 1870s.
Brighton Borough c.1875.
Brighton Branch of Borough 1863.
Brighton Branch of the Cliffe 1870-1879.
Brighton Branch of Commercial Square 1861-1862.
Buxted Bonfire Society.
Camberley c.1962/1966/1969?
Catsfield?
Chichester Bonfire Society 1800s, 1950s.
Chiddingfold Bonfire Society.
Clapham and Patching Bonfire Club 1952-2005.
Clayton [and Keymer] c.1887.
Cooksbridge Bonfire Society?
Crawley Bonfire Boys c.1877-1907?
Cripps Corner c.1908.
Denbigh Arms Bonfire Society (Bexhill) 1888.
Ditchling c.1949.
Eastbourne Bonfire Boys 1858-???
Eastbourne Boys of St. Marys c.1888.
Eastbourne Old Town Bonfire Society 1850s-??? 1950s-1966.

Eastbourne Seaside Boys.
East Grinstead.
Five Ashdown.
Frog and Duck Bonfire Society (Newhaven) 1983-1998.
Hadlow Down?
Hailsham Gala Association.
Hailsham Bonfire boys 1887, 1893.
Halland Bonfire Society c.1899.
Hampstead Bonfire Club.
Hassocks c.1949.
Hastings & St. Leonards Society c.1906.
Hastings Halton Bonfire Society.
Hastings & Ore Bonfire Society.
Haven Bonfire Society.
Hawkhurst c.1876.
Haywards Heath c. early 1970s.
Heathfield & District Bonfire Society 1950s.
Herstmonceux Bonfire Society.
Hitchin Bonfire Club (Hertfordshire).
Hollington (Hollington Wishing Tree Club) 1950s.
Hooe Bonfire Society 1980s, 1990s.
Horam Bonfire Society ???-1981.
Horsham Bonfire Society 1870-???
Hurstpierpoint c.1874-???, c.1900-1917.
Independents (Battle) 1878.
Jarvis Brook c.1890s/1990s.
Jolly Sailor Bonfire Society (Newhaven) c.1854.
Lewisham Bonfire Society (London).
Lingfield Bonfire Society (Surrey).
Little Common Bonfire Society (Bexhill) c.1878-early 1960s.
Mayfield c.1874.
Mountfield Bonfire Society.
Netherfield c.1907.
Newhaven c.1887.
Newhaven Carnival Society 1902-1999.

New Pound Bonfire Society.
Old Town Bonfire Society (Hastings) 1970.
Original Bonfire Boys (Rye) 1877.
Peasmarsh 1930s.
Pevensey c.1887.
Polegate Bonfire Association.
Portfield Community Association.
Ridgewood Bonfire Society 1933-2009/10.
Ringmer Bonfire Society c.1874, c.1887, c.1946.
Rodmell Bonfire Society.
Rotherfield c.1887.
Rye Bonfire Boys 1877.
St. Clements Bonfire Boys (Hastings) 1873.
St. Clements & West Hill Bonfire Boys (Hastings) 1949-1950.
St. Leonards Bonfire Society 1889.
Sedlescombe Bonfire Boys 1872.
Shamley Green Bonfire Boys Association.
Shere Bonfire Society.
Shoreham Bonfire Boys c. late 1870s, 1950s.
Shoreham-by-Sea Bonfire Association 1950s.
Sidley Bonfire Society 1890s-1990s.
Stones [sic] Cross 1890-1894?
Sussex Gypsy Bonfire Society 2004.
Terminus Place Bonfire Society c.1893.
The National Society (Hastings) [the same as Old Town Bonfire Society] 1889.
Ticehurst Bonfire Society 1890s.
Tivoli Bonfire Boys (Hastings) c.1875.
Tunbridge Wells c.1887.
Victorian Littlehampton Bonfire Society 1886-1905.
Vines Cross Bonfire Society c.1996-2007.
Waldron c.1902.
Westham Bonfire Society c.1893.
West Tarring Bonfire Society 1890s.
Worthing Bonfire Club c. late 1870s, 1893.

Worthing Bonfire Society c.1830s, c.1890, c.1955.
Worthing Loyal Torchlight Society 1863.

One other event that should not be overlooked, that being The Tar Barrels of Ottery. This is held each year on the 5th November in Ottery St Mary in Devon. Though not a bonfire society, they do have the tar barrels, but are not in costume. It is not known when this tradition started but probably after the gunpowder plot of 1605. This is not an event to be attended by the faint hearted.

******

Lewes Bonfire Society procession in 1853 by Thomas Hayward, the coloured painting is only display at Anne of Cleves House, Southover High Street, Lewes.

******

I would be very grateful to receive any additions, corrections etc. to these lists for inclusion in any reprint of this book, contact me at brianpugh140@btinternet.com

The Modern Version of Bonfire Prayers

Remember Remember
The Fifth of November,
The Gunpowder, Treason and Plot;
I see no reason
Why Gunpowder Treason
Should ever be forgot.
Guy Fawkes, Guy Fawkes,
'twas his intent
To blow up the King and the Parliament;
Three score barrels of powder below
Poor old England to overthrow;
By God's providence he was catch'd
With a dark lantern and burning match.
Holloa boys, holloa boys, make the bells ring
Holloa Boys, Holloa Boys, God save the King.

A penny loaf to feed the Pope,
A farthing o'cheese to choke him,
A pint of beer to rinse it down,
A faggot of sticks to burn him.
Burn him in a tub of tar,
Burn him like a blazing star,
Burn his body from his head,
Then we'll say old Pope is dead!
Hip, hip, hoo-r-r-ray!

******

Gunpowder Plot by Vernon Scannell

For days these curious cardboard buds have lain
In brightly coloured boxes. Soon the night
Will come. We pray there'll be no sullen rain
To make these magic orchids flame less bright.

Now in the garden's darkness they begin
To flower: the frenzied whizz of Catherine-wheel
Puts forth its fiery petals and the thin
Rocket soars too burst upon the steel

Bulwark of a cloud. And then the guy,
Absurdly human phoenix, is again
Gulped by greedy flames: the harvest sky
Is flecked with threshed and glittering golden grain.

'Uncle! A cannon! Watch me as I light it!"
The women helter-skelter, squealing high,
Retreat; the paper fuse is quickly lit,
A cat-like hiss, and spit of fire, a sly

Falter, then the air is shocked with blast,
The cannon bangs and in my nostrils drifts
A bitter scent that brings the lurking past
Lurching to my side. The present shofts,

Allows a ten-year memory to walk
Unhindered now; and so I'm forced to hear
The banshee howl of mortar and the talk
Of men who died, am forced to taste my fear.

I listen for a moment to the guns,
The torn earth's grunts, recalling how I prayed.
The past retreats. I hear a corpse's sons –
'Who's scared of bangers!' 'Uncle! John's afraid!'

THE LEWES ROUSER
Requiem for an old banger that died hard

East Sussex News, November 8, 1907
Written by SQUIB, bemoaning the banning of that famous Lewes banger.

Time was when, in the minds of men,
I were a thing of joy untold.
My memories ring when I reigned as king
In the bygone days of old.

Oh! I whizzed through the night, in a fiery flight,
Right in the midst of the fray,
Into the throng, scurrying along,
I wound my sinuous way.

I scattered the mud like the flying scud,
I leapt through the firelit space,
Belching sparks, leaving my marks,
I darted from place to place

See, the maidens fly with a frightened cry;
I laugh at their great distress.
But the faster they run, the greater the fun,
For my unwelcome attentions I press.

On the County Hall my sparks would fall
On the maid of justice frail,
By the Bishop's face I would madly race,
Leaving a blazing trail.

Away I would dart to the old White Hart,
Scattering the mob far and near;
Then back with a rush into the crush
I banged out my mad career.

Now an empty shuck, I lay in the ruck,
A victim to bigot and spleen;
Despite all entreats I'm barred from the streets,
The streets where my home once had been.

Though my glory is past, my memories may last
And be sung by poet and bard,
Remember, remember, oh boys of November
That I at least died hard.

******

1605 and Since

Oh! in ye yeare sixteen nought five
On ye fifth day of Novembre,
Was planned a dark and desperate deed
Which we should all remembre.
Ye plotte it was to kill ye King,
With his Parliament around him;
Ye plotter tho' was caught and foiled,
And with strong cords they bound him.
He met a well-deserved fate
'Midst general execration,
For all good men such evil deeds
Do hold in destestation.
And now in Lewes town each year
Is held a celebration,
Of ye King's escape, and ye plotte that failed,
And ye miscreant's frustration.
And so we sing God Save ye King!
And give God thanks that we
Who dwell in Merrie England
From Popish bonds are free.

Lewes, November 1911   W.C.
From the East Sussex News Friday, November, 3, 1911.

SUSSEX BY THE SEA.
By William Ward-Higgs 1907.

Now is the time for marching,
Now let your hearts be gay,
Hark to the merry bugles
Sounding along our way.
So let your voices ring, my boys,
And take the time from me,
And I'll sing you a song as we march along,
Of Sussex by the Sea!

Chorus
For we're the men from Sussex,
Sussex by the Sea.
We plough and sow and reap and mow,
And useful men are we;
And when you go to Sussex,
Whoever you may be,
You may tell them all that we stand and fall
For Sussex by the Sea!

Refrain
Oh Sussex, Sussex by the Sea!
Good old Sussex by the Sea!
You may tell them all that we stand or fall,
For Sussex by the Sea!

Up in the morning early,
Start at the break of day;
March till the evening shadows
Tell us its time to stay.
We're always moving on, my boys,
So take the time from me,
And sing this song as we march along,
Of Sussex by the Sea!

Chorus & Refrain

Sometimes your feet are weary,
Sometime the way is long,
Sometimes the day is dreary,
Sometimes the world goes wrong;
But if you let your voices ring,
Your care will fly away,
So we'll sing a song as we march along,
Of Sussex by the Sea!

Chorus & Refrain

Light is the love of a soldier,
That's what the ladies say-
Lightly he goes a wooing,
Lightly he rides away.
In love and war we always are
As fair as fair can be,
And a soldier boy is the ladies joy
In Sussex by the Sea!

Chorus & Refrain

Far o'er the seas we wonder,
Wide thro' the world we roam:
Far from the kind hearts yonder,
Far from our dear old home;
But ne'er shall we forget, my boys,
And true we'll ever be
To the girls so kind that we left behind
In Sussex by the Sea!

Chorus & Refrain

******

Sussex Won't be Druv
By W. Victor Cook

Some folks as comes to Sussex,
They rackons as they knows
A darn sight better what to do
Then silly folks like me and you
Could possibly suppose.
But them as comes to Sussex,
They mustn't push and shove'
For Sussex will be Sussex,
And Sussex won't be druv.

All folks as comes to Sussex
Must follow Sussex ways,
And when they've larned to know us well
There's no place else they'd wish to dwell
In all their blessed days.
There ant no place like Sussex
Until you goos above,
But Sussex will be Sussex,
And Sussex won't be druv!

******

Sources
Burchfield, John & Cooper, Richard, *Fifty Years of Fire: A History of Littlehampton Bonfire Society*, [Chichester, Sussex: Phillimore & Co. Ltd., 2003].
Cliffe Bonfire Society Archives.
Etherington, Jim, *Lewes Bonfire Night*, [Seaford, Sussex: S.B. Publications, 1993, 1994 & revised and reprinted 2001].
East Sussex County Council Minute Books of the Roads & Bridges Committee Meetings March-November 1961 & January-July 1962.
Fisk, Michael S, *Nevill Juvenile Bonfire Society*, (Privately Printed 1979).
Laker, June, *The East Hoathly & Halland Carnival Society* [East Hoathly, Sussex: CTR Publishing, 2001].
Lewes Bonfire Council Minutes 1957-72, 1972-76 & 1976-79.
Munt, Bert, *Lewes Bonfires:* 121 page scrapbook, hardback album containing handbills, programmes and press cuttings.
The Tar Barrels of Ottery, 2010 Souvenir Programme.
Various Society programmes and web sites from Cliffe, Borough, Commercial, Waterloo, South Street, Nevill and Southover.
The Viva Lewes Handbook November 2006, issue 2.

Further Reading
Brimacombe, Peter, *Guy Fawkes and the Gunpowder Plot*, (London: Pitkin Publishing, 2005).
Chapman, Brigid, *Night Of The Fires,* (Seaford: S.B. Publications, 1994).
Etherington, Jim, *Bonfire: The Lewes Bonfire Societies in Photographs,* (Seaford: S.B. Publications, 1997).
Foxworthy, Tony, *Customs in Sussex*, (Derbyshire: Country Books, 2011).
Fraser, Antonia, *The Gunpowder Plot: Terror & Faith in*

1605, (London: Mandarin Books, 1997).

Goring, Jeremy, *Burn Holy Fire: Religion in Lewes since the Reformation*, (Cambridge: London: The Lutterworth Press, 2003).

Hoad, M.A., *400 and still burning: A History of the Battle Bonfire & the Bonfire Boyes*, (Leicester: Troubador Publishing Ltd., 2007).

Longley, R.A. *Battel Bonfire Boyes: Bangers, Bloomers & Bonfire: A Light Hearted Look at the Battel Bonfire Boyes*, (St. Leonards-on-Sea: Longley Esq., 1997).

Malam, John, *The Gunpowder Plot* [Dates with History], (London: Cherrytree Books, 2003).

Sharpe, James, *Remember Remember the Fifth of November*, (London: Profile Books, 2005).

Stoneham, E.T., *Sussex Martyrs of the Reformation*, (Worthing, Sussex: Henry E. Walter Ltd., 1967).

Thomas, Andy, *Street of Fire,* (Seaford: S.B. Publications, 1999).

Thomas, Andy, *Lewes on the Fifth,* (Seaford: S.B. Publications, 2008).

Various Authors, *Gunpowder Plot: A Celebration of 400 Years of Bonfire Night*, (London: Penguin Books, 2005).

******

About the Author Brian William Pugh

Brian W. Pugh is an author with a particular interest the Lewes Bonfire Celebrations. He was born in Lewes, Sussex during 1944 and was educated at Western Road Primary School, Lewes and Mountfield Road County Secondary School, Lewes, he has lived in Lewes all of his life and is semi-retired.

Having lived in Western Road in his early years, he enjoyed watching the Borough Bonfire Society processions in that area of the town, he remembers as a very young lad being fascinated by Ted Over and the Zulus. In later years he joined the Cliffe Bonfire Society and was a member for many years, taking part as a cavalier and carrying one of the many banners. Even though he has not been a member of Cliffe or any other society for some time, he maintains a keen interest in the celebrations of all the societies and may the tradition continue for many years.

His other interest is Sir Arthur Conan Doyle, his life and published works; he is the Curator of The Conan Doyle (Crowborough) Establishment a society dedicated to Arthur Conan Doyle.

He is the author of *A Chronology of the Life of Sir Arthur Conan Doyle* [privately printed, 2000], *The Sir Arthur Conan Doyle Statue At Crowborough* [privately printed, 2001], *Buzzin In Sussex: An Investigation Into The Connections Of Sir Arthur Conan Doyle, His Family And Sherlock Holmes* [privately printed, 2005], *A Chronology of the Life of Sir Arthur Conan Doyle* [London: MX Publishing 2009] and as joint author with John Hackworth, *The Conan Doyle Crowborough Walk* [privately printed, 2005]. He is also joint author with Paul

R. Spiring of *On The Trail of Arthur Conan Doyle: An Illustrated Devon Tour* [Brighton: Book Guild Publishing Ltd, 2008], *Auf der Spur von Arthur Conan Doyle* [Mannheim: Dryas Verlag, 2008], *Bertram Fletcher Robinson: A Footnote to The Hound of the Baskervilles* [London: MX Publishing, 2008], *Tras las huellas de Arthur Conan Doyle* [London: MX Publishing, 2008] and *Arthur Conan Doyle, Sherlock Holmes and Devon: A Complete Tour Guide & Companion* [London: MX Publishing, 2010] with Paul Spiring and Sadru Bhanji. He has had a number of articles printed in various Sherlock Holmes society journals and edits The Conan Doyle (Crowborough) Establishment Newsletter and The Annual Birthday File. He also gives guided walks in Crowborough, visiting various sites that are connected with ACD; he has been frequently interviewed on live radio programmes and has featured on various television programmes connected with ACD.

Photograph by Edward Reeves, Lewes

Index of Persons

Adams, M 76
Alexander III of Russia 102
Alexandra, Princess 160
Allen, W R (Bob) 147, 162
Amy, Novice 64
Amey, Philip 154, 155
Andrewes, Lancelot of 74
Anne of Cleves 123, 179
Armitage, John 162, 168
Ashdown, Ann 21, 126
Austria, Emperor of (Effigy) 93, 94
Avington, Thomas 21, 126

Bacon, Mr Peter 43, 63, 85, 95
Baker MP, Mr Norman 167
Banana Bill (W H Penfold) 148, 153, 158
Banks, Mr William 12, 21, 22, 25, 34, 74, 136
Bassett, Malcolm 166
Bates, Thomas 25, 126
Beard, Mr Charles 134
Beckett, Arthur 26, 50, 57, 62, 73, 74, 107
Beeching, Mr F 20
Betty, Old 46
Blackman, Mr 16, 24, 37, 83, 131
Bomba, King (King of Naples) (Effigy) 99
Bosher, Mr 141
Brimacombe, Peter 187
Brock, Messrs C T 21, 32, 136
Brooks, Mr John 163
Brougham, Lord, 5
Bryant, Arthur 54
Burchfield, John 187
Burgess, Denis 21, 126
Burgess, Frank W 23

Cameron, David 168
Carver, Dirick 21, 126
Catesby, Robert 25, 126, 127, 146, 149
Chapman, Brigid 171, 187
Charles I, King 74
Charles II, King 54
Chatfield, Mr E 17
Chichester, Bishop of 74, 96
Chichester, Lord 6, 17, 19, 39, 41, 57, 58, 84, 85, 87, 131
China, Emperor of (Effigy) 98
Clegg, Nick 168
Cole, G D H 81
Colvin, Mr F 2
Connaught, Duke and Duchess of 138
Connell, J M 74
Cook, W Victor 186
Cooper, Richard 187
Cruse, Harry 122

Danvers-Walker, Bob 154
Davis, Mrs M 48
Dawe, Eli 66, 106
Delhi, King of (Effigy) 96
Digby, Everard 25, 126
Disney, Walt 152
Durham, Bishop of 89

Earl, Charlie 154, 167
Earl, Peter 154, 155
Earl, Wendy 155
Edmunds, Christina (Effigy) 136
Edward VII, King 141
Elizabeth I, Queen 54, 73
Elizabeth II, Queen 116, 151, 158, 159, 165
Ellman, Mr 79
Ellman, Mr John 20, 42, 60, 88

Ellman, The Reverend Edmund Boys 79
Emmanuel, Victor (Effigy) 99
Etherington, Jim 187
Evelyn 74

Faux, Guy 1, 127
Fawkes, Guido 23, 24, 25, 28, 53, 56, 70, 73, 86, 87, 126
Fawkes, Guy (Effigy) 29, 34, 63, 73, 91, 92, 93, 105, 109, 112, 114, 119, 121, 126, 132, 137, 138, 146, 149, 150, 163, 167
Fisk, Michael S 187
Flanigan, Supt. 15, 36, 56, 82, 130
Flint, Mr Benjamin 60, 132
Flood, Father 164
Foxworthy, Tony 187
Fraser, Antonia 187
Frazer, Sir James 72

Gage, Lord 80
Garibaldi, Giuseppe (Banner) 99
Garibaldi, Giuseppe (Effigy) 64
Gearing, Thomas Ernest 66, 106
Gearing, Tom 119
Gearing, William Thomas 66, 106
George III, King 84
George V, King 142, 144, 145
George VI, King 147, 148
Gloucester, Duke of 146
Godfrey, Sir Edmunbury (Representation) 1
Goering, Hermann (Effigy) 113, 115
Goring, Jeremy 188
Grant, John 25, 126
Groves, Mary 21, 126
Gwynn, Denis 61

Harberd 94

Harding, Gilbert 152
Hardy, Thomas (Quote) 71, 115
Harland, Thomas 21, 126
Harris, Benjamin 1, 127
Hayward, Thomas 179
Hillman, Mr John 14
Hillman, Mr T 17
Hitler, Adolf 112, 146
Hoad, M A 188
Holman, John 55, 129
Hosman, Alexander 21, 126
Huggett, Mr W 67

James, E O 72
James I, King 28, 53, 70, 73, 89, 126
James II, King 34, 54, 55, 73

Kaiser Bill (Tableau) 110
Keyes, Robert 25, 126
Khan, Genghis 155

Laker, June 187
Lichfield, Patrick, 160
Lloyd, Fatty 122
Longley, R.A., 188
Lower, Mark Anthony (An Old Inhabitant) 3, 11, 37, 38, 56, 57, 84

Mackay, Captain 18, 40, 57
Mainard, William 21, 126
Malam, John 188
Manning, Archbishop (Effigy) 136
Mantell, Dr. (Quote) 23
Mary, Queen 142, 145
McCrimmon, Donald 125
Moloch 26, 30

Morris, Mr 17
Morris, Mr 80
Morris, James 21, 126
Morris, Margery 21, 126
Munt, Bill 49
Munt, Christine 49
Munt, Doris 48
Munt, Ron 48
Munt, Mr Sydney Albert (Bert) 48, 49, 50, 118, 152, 187
Murrell, Dr.134
Mussolini, Benito (Effigy) 112, 146
Myles, Thomas 21, 126

Naples, King of (Effigy) 99
Napoleon, Louis (Effigy) 99
Neal, Mr 19
Neale, Reverend J M 64, 96, 97, 98
Newton, Bishop of (Effigy) 93
Nicholl, Dr. Pat 162

Oates, Titus 54, 127
O'Connell 83, 131
Ogilvy, Hon. Angus 160
O'Halloran, Simon 70
Old Betty 46
Old Father Time (Tableau) 164
Orange, William of 55, 67, 68, 69, 78, 79, 119, 128
Oswald, John 21, 126
Over, Mr Edward (Ted) 160, 190
Owen, Hugh 126

Paisley, Ian 160
Penfold, W H (Banana Bill) 148, 153, 158
Pepys, Samuel 54
Percy, Thomas 25, 126, 127
Pettitt, Annette 122

Philips, David 49
Philips, Dorothy 48
Playford, Fred 155
Plimsoll MP, Samuel 138
Plunkett, William 78
Pope Leo XIII (Effigy) 138
Pope Paul V (Effigy) 68, 105, 114, 119, 121, 122, 146, 148, 149, 159
Pope Pius IX (Effigy) 61, 64, 89, 92, 100, 132, 135
Portsmouth, Countess of 141
Postgate, R 81
Povey, S 148
Prussia, King of (Effigy) 93, 94
Pusey, Dr. 96

Quinn, David 167

Red Riding Hood (Tableau) 112
Reed, Thomas 21, 126
Reeves, Edward 190
Richardson, The Reverend W E 103, 140
Richmond, His Grace, the Duke of 6
Rookwood, Ambrose 25, 126
Russell, Lord John 61, 89
Russia, Alexander III of 102
Russia, Czar of 134
Russia, Czar of (Effigy) 92
Russia, Emperor of (Effigy) 93, 94

Sawyer, John 23
Saxby, Mr H 17
Scannell, Vernon 76, 82, 99, 110, 181
Scobell, Miss 96
Scobell, The Reverend John 96
Shakespeare, William (Quote) 3
Sharpe, James 188

Shiffner, (Bart), Sir Henry 17, 39, 57, 85
Smart, Mr 19
Spilsbury, Mr 77
Squib, 182
Stevens, George 21, 126
Stevenson, Michael 160
Stoneham, E T 188

Taylor, Aubrey 148, 166
Teck, Princess May of 140
Thomas, Andy 188
Tresham, Francis 25, 126, 127

Verrell, Annette Philly 119
Victor, Prince Albert 135
Victoria, Queen 61, 89, 94, 139, 140

Ward-Higgs, William 184
Washer, Mrs Kate 123
Watkins, E I 89
Weston, Harold 66, 106
Wheeler, Tom 142, 158
Whistler, Laurance 53
Whitfield, Mr 14, 130
Wille, junior, Mr 17
William of Orange 55, 67, 68, 69, 79, 119, 128
Williams, Francis 59
Williams, Mr Frank R 56
Winter, Eric 165
Winter, Martin 168
Winter, Nathan 168
Winter, Robert 25, 126
Winter, Thomas 25, 126
Wiseman, Cardinal 61, 63, 89, 90, 132
Wood, Mr G 17
Wood, Thomas 21, 126

Wood, Thomasina 126
Woodman, Richard 2, 21, 126
Wright, Christopher 25, 126, 127
Wright, John 25, 126, 127
Wright, Ron 152, 157

York, Duke of 140

Also from MX Publishing, some of the leading Sherlock Holmes and Arthur Conan Doyle writers from the UK and USA, including the bestselling:

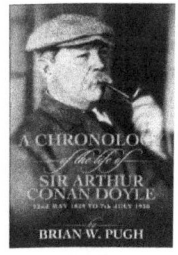

The Chronology of Arthur Conan Doyle

The definitive chronology used by historians and libraries worldwide.

Close To Holmes

A Look at the Connections Between Historical London, Sherlock Holmes and Sir Arthur Conan Doyle.

…… and many more available from all good bookstores, Amazon Kindle, Kobo Books, iTunes and other formats.

www.mxpublishing.com

www.ingramcontent.com/pod-product-compliance
Lightning Source LLC
Chambersburg PA
CBHW071705090426
42738CB00009B/1664